Woodworker's Joint Book

The Complete Guide to Wood Joinery

TERRIE NOLL

APPLE

A QUARTO BOOK

First published in the United Kingdom
by the Apple Press
Sheridan House, 112–116a Western Road
Hove, East Sussex BN3 1DD

ISBN 1-84092-422-5

QUAR.JOBO

Conceived, designed, and produced by
Quarto Publishing plc
The Old Brewery
6 Blundell Street
London N7 9BH

QUAR.JOBO

Project Editor: Nadia Naqib
Senior Art Editor: Penny Cobb
Designer: Paul Griffin
Illustrators: Ed Roberts, Lawrie Taylor,
Kevin Maddison, Terry Hadler,
George Fryer
Technical Advisor: Phillip Gardner
Joint Constructor: William Powell
Photographers: Paul Forrester, Colin Bowling
Text Editors: Ian Kearey, Alan Richmond
Indexer: Pamela Ellis

Art Director: Moira Clinch
Publisher: Piers Spence

Manufactured by
Pica Digital PTE Ltd, Singapore
Printed by Midas Printing
International Ltd., China

9 8 7 6 5 4 3 2

Contents

CHAPTER FIVE
Mortise-and-Tenon

CHAPTER SIX
Miters and Bevels

CHAPTER SEVEN
Dovetails

CHAPTER EIGHT
Dowels and Biscuits

CHAPTER NINE
Fasteners, Hardware, and Knockdown Joints

Measuring and marking

Measuring out a given distance and marking it precisely onto wood is a simple task provided certain rules are applied. These ensure that the fine tolerances of joinery (within the thickness of one or two business cards) are accurately laid out on the workpiece using the basic tools of pencil, awl, and marking knife.

As a pencil point dulls, its mark becomes wider and less precise. An awl mark is consistently narrow, but produces a fuzzy line when scribing cross-grain. A marking knife makes the finest line possible and avoids introducing slop into the joint.

Scribing cross-grain with a marking knife cleanly severs the top layer of wood fibers, and helps to prevent tear-out (losing bits of wood from the surface). It also leaves a tiny clean cut to guide tools. A good marking knife has a fine-tapered cross-section and a long tip to get into corners, like that on some chip carving knives.

Even the finest line has no value unless it is precisely placed. Etched increments in a ruler help to locate the tip of a marking knife precisely at the increment. Holding a ruler on edge so the increment contacts the wood will avoid inaccuracies.

Steel tapes and rulers vary in quality. Buying within one brand helps, especially if one tape is used for larger parts and a short, lighter one for the smaller work. Check that the measurements match.

Gauges

Marking and cutting gauges are layout tools that scribe a line parallel to a wood edge with a steel point or knife. A moveable fence adjusts the line's distance from the edge. Special mortise marking gauges scribe two parallel lines to help lay out the mortise-and-tenon or other joints. The distance between their two points is adjustable, and so is their fence. All these tools need to be fine-tuned. Careful selection avoids the inconveniences of poor design that lead to difficult or inaccurate fence and point settings.

Incremental Markings

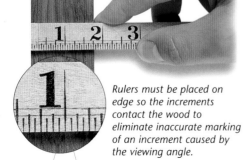

Rulers must be placed on edge so the increments contact the wood to eliminate inaccurate marking of an increment caused by the viewing angle.

Extend all metal tapes and rulers and compare whether their increments align and their lengths at full extension are the same.

Marking Tools

The lines made by different marking devices can vary in width and affect the accuracy of the layout.

Scribing knife makes finest line.

Marking awl marks well with the grain.

Pencil lines vary with sharpness.

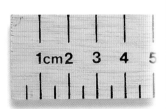

Avoid wooden rulers whose increments are painted rather than incised, as the increments themselves are too wide to be accurate.

Marking and Cutting Gauges

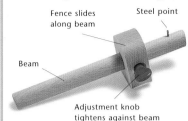

Fence slides along beam

Steel point

Beam

Adjustment knob tightens against beam

A basic marking gauge has a round steel point and adjustable fence that rides the wood's edge while the point marks a line a set distance from the edge.

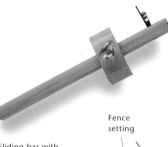

A cutting gauge has a small knife wedged into the beam and is good for clean cross-grain scoring in addition to cutting narrow strips of veneer.

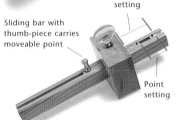

Sliding bar with thumb-piece carries moveable point

Fence setting

Point setting

The mortise gauge's fixed and moveable points mark parallel lines, but on this model, the fence and point settings have to be held until one knob tightens them.

A thumbscrew moves the point up and down the beam, but the screw adjustment that tightens the fence needs another tool to tighten it.

A thumbscrew on this gauge sets the distance between points, and a second knob tightens the fence setting to locate the parallel lines in the wood.

Squares and angles

Squareness in woodworking is the basis for smoothly working doors and drawers and tight-fitting joinery. An accurate square could be the most important tool a woodworker owns. Unfortunately, in today's tool market, quality is quite varied and not all squares are square.

"You get what you pay for" is especially pertinent when it comes to layout tools. Woodworkers can select among the glittery wood and brass woodworker's squares or cross over to the sterile precision of high-tolerance machinist tools.

Except for one or two expensive brand names dedicated to precision, few wood and brass squares are exact and may be square only on their inside corner. Brand name engineer's combination squares are expensive, but they are square within one- or two-thousandths in 12" (30 cm) of blade. They also have more versatility than woodworker's squares. Even the simplest patternmaker's double square with a sliding blade also functions as a marking gauge, a depth gauge, a mini-level, and a height gauge, so it offers more value. Most hardware stores sell combination squares cheaply modeled after engineering tools.

Squares can be tested before buying and corrected like any other tool. Expensive brands that go out of square are worth returning to the factory for adjustment. Manufacturers of less expensive tools don't offer that service, and the tools have to be adjusted in the shop.

Angle Tools

The basic tool for laying out angles is the T-bevel, or sliding bevel. It is set to match a drafted or existing angle to transfer it to a part or machine. Since the object is to have a variable tool angle, precision isn't an issue unless the blade or beam isn't straight. There are several different bevel designs, such as the bevel square's fixed blade and the sliding bevel's moveable one, plus different methods for tightening the setting. All are matters of preference and ease of use.

Architect's triangles aren't particularly expensive but are accurate enough to provide a reference standard in the shop. They are needed for accurate drawings, and can also be utilized to help set bevels or other tools.

Aids to Accuracy and Order

Squares for Woodworking

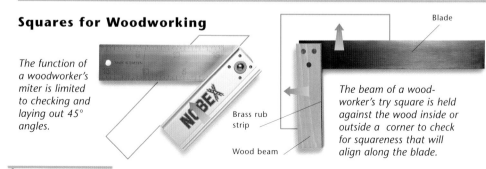

The function of a woodworker's miter is limited to checking and laying out 45° angles.

Brass rub strip

Wood beam

Blade

The beam of a woodworker's try square is held against the wood inside or outside a corner to check for squareness that will align along the blade.

Tools for Laying out Angles

The blade and beam of a bevel square pivot from a joint at the end.

Using a screw to tighten the sliding bevel blade keeps interference to a minimum, but the screwdriver has to be kept close at hand.

A sliding T-bevel allows the blade to extend to different lengths, but lever or wing nut tighteners can extend outside the beam and get in the way.

A wing nut at the end of a sliding bevel's beam conveniently tightens the blade and doesn't interfere with setting or transferring angles.

Adjustable and fixed-angle architect's triangles are accurate enough for setting up machines and laying out angles.

The combination head of an engineer's square can be supplemented by a protractor head for setting out angles and a center head, which locates the center of cylinders.

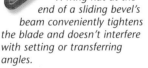

The patternmaker's version, with a sliding blade and bubble level, checks for squareness inside and out.

A woodworker's miter square and engineer's combination square both check squares and miters for accuracy, but the combination square's sliding blade makes it a depth and marking gauge too.

Squares and Angles

7

Exact clamping and assembly

Despite good craftsmanship, the fit of joinery can be distorted by mis-directed clamp forces. A great deal of time and energy has been invested by the time the parts are ready for gluing, but a little more patience spent on careful clamping pays off.

Aids to Accuracy and Order

Glued parts will slip or assemblies distort if the bearing surfaces of the clamps aren't square to the wood, and the clamp's length is not parallel to the nearest wood surface. Clamping wood is like pressing a finger into a sponge: if the wood is too thin to distribute the force, or too few clamps are used, then the area around the pressure point may deflect, losing the contact necessary for a good bond.

Clamping blocks cut from scrap help to solve this problem by distributing the pressure and, in the process, prevent the clamp from marring the wood surface. But clamping blocks can make the problem worse if they aren't sized to the thickness, width, or area of the joint being glued.

Dry Testing

Dry test the fit of all assemblies before any glue is applied. This way, last minute refitting will be less messy or rushed by drying glue. The dry test gives you the opportunity to decide on the clamps needed, cut the clamping blocks, and have the glue and other materials close at hand. Don't forget spreading rollers or brushes, waxed paper to insert between blocks and wood, and clean-up rags.

Once clamped, check the assembly for squareness while the wet glue still allows for adjustment. This is done by measuring the diagonals with a tape or diagonal sticks (see opposite). Once the diagonals measure the same, the assembly is square.

Distributing Pressure

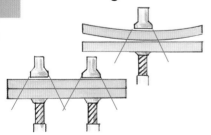

When the wood is thin or there aren't enough clamps, the pressure isn't distributed evenly and may cause the surrounding wood parts to separate.

Positioning Clamps

The bearing surfaces of the clamps need to be flat to the wood and in line so pressure won't distort an assembly or cause it to slide out of position.

Pressure pads in line

Clamp leg and material parallel

Checking Assemblies for Square

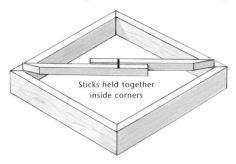

Sticks held together inside corners

An assembly is square if the diagonals between inside corners match, whether measured from the tape's inch mark to the corner diagonally opposite or by diagonal sticks extended between the corners.

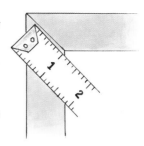

Measure from inch mark diagonally to opposite inside corners

Sizing and Placing Blocks

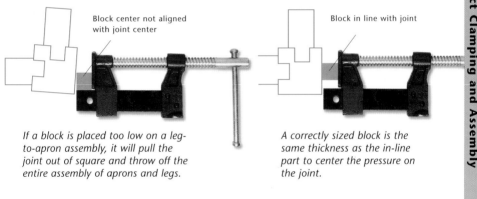

Block center not aligned with joint center

Block in line with joint

If a block is placed too low on a leg-to-apron assembly, it will pull the joint out of square and throw off the entire assembly of aprons and legs.

A correctly sized block is the same thickness as the in-line part to center the pressure on the joint.

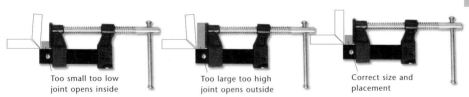

Too small too low joint opens inside

Too large too high joint opens outside

Correct size and placement

Clamping blocks distribute the pressure and prevent marring, but a block that is too narrow and placed too low will open the joint on the inside.

A thick block that extends above the thickness of the joint will push it in on itself and open the outside corners.

Raising the block brings the clamp pressure in line with the apron for a square assembly.

The basic orientations of wood parts

In any design where the parts meet in common configurations, ways are developed to hold them together mechanically, with adhesive, or by a combination of the two. The positional relationships of the parts are not in themselves joints, but certain families of joints and joint types evolve from these basic orientations to meet the requirements of the material, the structure, and the aesthetics.

Parallel Orientation

Boards joined by their edges to increase overall wood width are in the parallel orientation. It permits using narrow stock, as well as the division and reassembly of wide stock to minimize checking and cupping. Parallel orientation also offers the flexibility to enhance design with grain patterns, which are more properly described as the wood's "figures."

I Orientation

When wood is joined end to end in the I orientation, the overall wood length is increased. Scarf joints have evolved from the I orientation and are widely used in timber framing. The scarf joint is common to boat building, but it only occasionally appears in furniture, where it is used either in utility or in decoration.

Crossed Orientation

The crossed orientation has a small family of face-to-face lap joints doing light-duty joining of frames. Chinese latticework has made an art form of this orientation. By contrast, the deeper edge lap has limited use and refinement. It is primarily seen in knockdown plywood construction or in egg-crated drawer dividers.

L Orientation

The L orientation is the most common for carcass, corner, and framing joints. There are three ways wood can be joined in the L orientation: end to edge, end to face, and edge to face. Reinforced butts and miters, mortise and tenon, lap joints, box or finger joints, rabbets, the dovetail and more are all generated at this corner.

T Orientation

This orientation spawns mortise-and-tenon and lap joints, but is best thought of as the site of the housed joint, whether dadoed, rabbeted, or dovetailed. T joints can be end to edge, end to face, or edge to face.

Angled Orientation

The angled orientation acts as a modifier to the other orientations. It picks and chooses members from various joint families as it mixes with each positional orientation, changing the joining angle to anything other than 90° or 180°. Hence we have such joints as the oblique scarf, angled lap, and barrel stave construction.

The joints listed opposite can be developed if the wood you are working with is in the orientation shown.

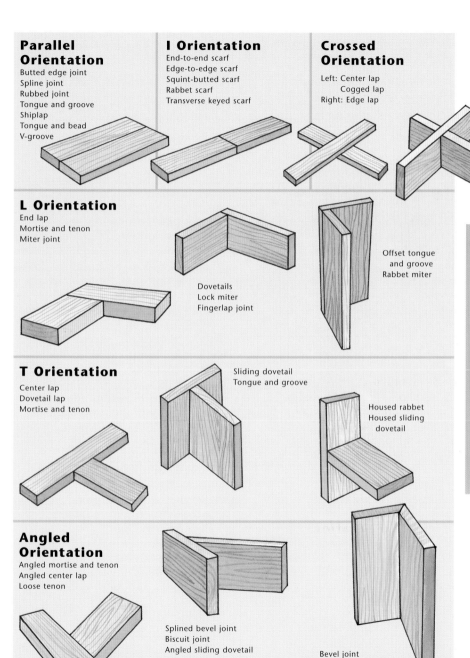

Parallel Orientation

Butted edge joint
Spline joint
Rubbed joint
Tongue and groove
Shiplap
Tongue and bead
V-groove

I Orientation

End-to-end scarf
Edge-to-edge scarf
Squint-butted scarf
Rabbet scarf
Transverse keyed scarf

Crossed Orientation

Left: Center lap
       Cogged lap
Right: Edge lap

L Orientation

End lap
Mortise and tenon
Miter joint

Dovetails
Lock miter
Fingerlap joint

Offset tongue
and groove
Rabbet miter

T Orientation

Center lap
Dovetail lap
Mortise and tenon

Sliding dovetail
Tongue and groove

Housed rabbet
Housed sliding
dovetail

Angled Orientation

Angled mortise and tenon
Angled center lap
Loose tenon

Splined bevel joint
Biscuit joint
Angled sliding dovetail

Bevel joint
Splined bevel joint

The elements of joinery

Each woodworking joint is a combination of at least two basic elements that are mated and mechanically interlock, or create glue surfaces that "join" two parts. As joinery gets more complex, the elements are modified and enhanced to improve joint strength or design, but the basic components remain the same.

Elements fall roughly into two categories. Sawn elements can be completed by one cut on the wood's end or edge by a hand or power saw. Milled elements are part of a process that begins with sizing the part, then removes material to leave a characteristic shape cut into the wood.

A sawn element—square, angled, or compound angled—is butted to its complementary cut to make width joints, mitered corners, six-sided boxes, and so on. Although these shapes are usually made by sawing, they may also be achieved by hand planing, power joining, or routing.

Milled elements

These include the L-shaped rabbet, variously shaped pockets or sockets, and U-shaped groove, dado, and edge dado or notch. These flat-bottomed, U-shaped cuts are distinguished by whether they parallel the grain (groove), cross the grain (dado), or cut into the board's edge (notch). Different joint families combine these with other cuts to form joints suited to the design—the square cut and pocket yields a mortise-and-tenon joint; a dado and square cut gives the housing joint for shelves; a rabbet and dado create a lap joint for T-joining parts, and so on.

Milled and sawn cuts can be made in an infinite number of ways. In fact, knowing how to make them by a variety of tools and means, how to modify them, and how to combine them with other elements is what joinery is all about.

Sawn Elements

Square cuts result when the blade angle is 90° to the wood surface and the blade path runs 90° to the entrance end or edge of the wood.

In an angled cut, either the blade angle is not 90° to the wood surface or the blade path doesn't run 90° to the entrance plane.

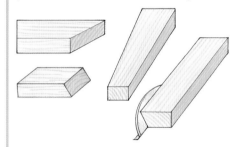

In a compound angle, both the blade angle and blade path are not 90°. They are any other angle or combination of blade angle and blade path.

Designing Joints

Milled Elements

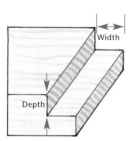

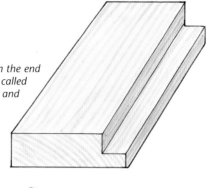

An L-shaped step cut in the end or edge of the wood is called a rabbet, whose depth and width can be varied as needed.

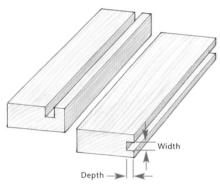

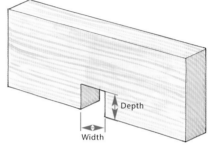

Grooves are flat-bottomed, U-shaped cuts that always run parallel to the grain in the face or edge of the wood.

A dado cut into the edge of a board is called a notch or edge dado and is usually deeper than a dado cut in the board face.

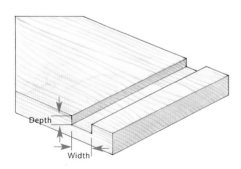

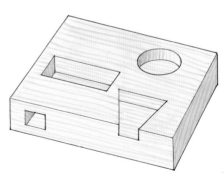

A dado is also a U-shaped flat-bottomed cut like a groove, but dadoes only run across the grain and, if cut wide, are sometimes called trenches.

Pockets vary in shape and in their location in the board, have specialized names, and serve different joinery purposes, which are covered in following chapters.

Wood material and joint design

The most important fact to keep in mind when designing wood joinery is that solid wood is not dimensionally stable. The cell structure of wood can be likened simplistically to a bundle of straws, which absorb and expel water vapor in response to changes in the relative humidity to maintain moisture equilibrium with the environment. This constant fluctuation of the wood's moisture content results in expansion and contraction across the width of grain and a negligible change in length. Unless this phenomenon is addressed by design, it's possible for wood movement to destroy a joint or the material itself.

Designing Joints

Predicting Wood Movement

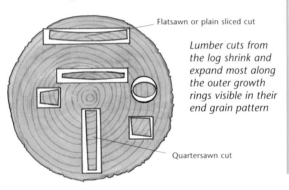

Flatsawn or plain sliced cut

Lumber cuts from the log shrink and expand most along the outer growth rings visible in their end grain pattern

Quartersawn cut

Movement

Wood movement becomes a danger to joinery when the long grain of one part is joined across the grain of another, and dimensional conflict arises. This situation is found in some of the L, T, and crossed positions where the long grain of two parts meet at right angles.

Movement in wood varies by species, by its classification

Grain and Wood Movement

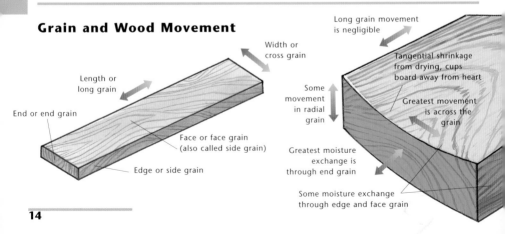

Long grain movement is negligible

Width or cross grain

Length or long grain

End or end grain

Face or face grain (also called side grain)

Edge or side grain

Some movement in radial grain

Greatest moisture exchange is through end grain

Tangential shrinkage from drying, cups board away from heart

Greatest movement is across the grain

Some moisture exchange through edge and face grain

as hardwood or softwood, and between the heartwood and sapwood of each tree. The key to predicting movement lies in the end grain of each board.

In relation to the growth rings of the tree, wood moves more tangentially than radially, or more along the rings than across them. As wet wood dries, tangential shrinkage distorts the board consistent with its original position in the log. That position is easy to determine by the pattern of growth rings in a board's end grain.

Flatsawn boards are usually cut so the growth rings on the end run more parallel to the width than the thickness of the board. Quartersawn boards are cut so growth rings are more perpendicular to the width of the board. The rule of thumb is that a flatsawn board will shrink twice as much across its width as a quartersawn board, and have twice the potential for expansion and dimensional instability.

Grain

With effort, wood can be broken across the grain, but the likelier breakage is along the grain when wood is left too thin or when weak "short grain" created by milling can't hold the material together. Conscientious design can reduce or eliminate all these problems.

Strength and Grain Design

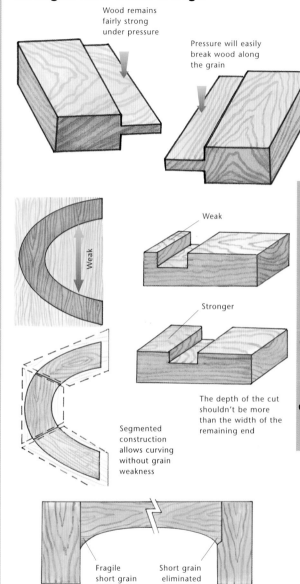

Wood remains fairly strong under pressure

Pressure will easily break wood along the grain

Weak

Weak

Stronger

The depth of the cut shouldn't be more than the width of the remaining end

Segmented construction allows curving without grain weakness

Fragile short grain

Short grain eliminated

Wood is fragile when the grain runs across a point created by a curved cut; a different joint design reduces the danger of breakage in arched door frames.

Strategies for Accommodating Wood Movement

Align grain to unify movement *Continuing the long grain around a carcass unifies wood movement. Keeping long grain vertical on the sides prevents shrinkage from binding doors. Running long grain across the bottom keeps shrinkage from tightening the drawers.*

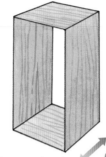

Cabinet expands and contracts across the grain as a unit

Design cross grain joints to eliminate conflict
The mechanical interlock of a sliding dovetail holds the breadboard end of a tabletop without glue. One central pin keeps the end aligned as the top moves freely with changes in humidity.

Movement of top from pin

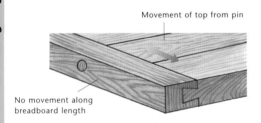

No movement along breadboard length

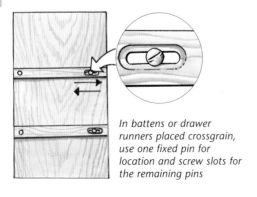

In battens or drawer runners placed crossgrain, use one fixed pin for location and screw slots for the remaining pins

Strategies for Minimizing Wood Movement

Arrange grain to reduce movement

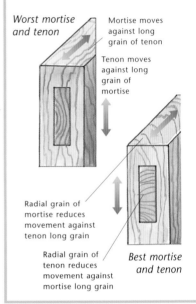

Worst mortise and tenon

Mortise moves against long grain of tenon

Tenon moves against long grain of mortise

Radial grain of mortise reduces movement against tenon long grain

Radial grain of tenon reduces movement against mortise long grain

Best mortise and tenon

Use the best of classic designs
Classic drawer design attaches a solid bottom to the front groove only. This allows wide grain to expand under the low back while air can escape over it to avoid pistoning when closing.

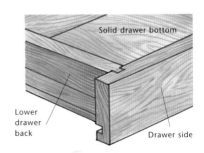

Solid drawer bottom

Lower drawer back

Drawer side

Select a stable species or cut

Pine

Rosewood

Plain cut

Quartersawn cut

An 18" (45 cm) width of new-growth pine can move as much as ⅜" (0.9 cm) more than a similar width of rosewood.

Generally the width of plain sliced or flatsawn lumber moves about twice the amount as quartersawn lumber of the same species.

Finish all sides equally to balance movement and reduce extremes of moisture exchange *Wood finished on only one side will cup from imbalanced moisture exchange with the environment.*

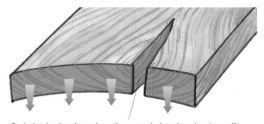

End checks develop when the unsealed end grain gives off moisture and shrinks more than the rest of the board

Strategies for Restraining Wood Movement

Increased bonding area helps the glue restrain movement

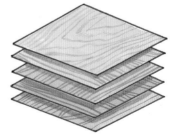

Divide and conquer
Glue will restrain wood movement if the glue surface area in the joint is high in relation to the wood thickness.

Play forces against each other
The alternating grain directions in layers of plywood combine to form a stable material. For information on wood movement and glue, see page 20.

Choosing a joint

One school of thought says a craftsperson should design around the construction; another says construct around the design. In reality both methods interact. The design dictates the possible joints or is modified to accommodate joints that will overcome the structure's weaknesses.

Before the basic orientations of wood are joined and put into service, the forces the joints have to resist need to be analyzed. This doesn't require an engineering degree, just an awareness of the mechanical stresses on joints and some solutions to them. Potential problems from stresses on an assembly in use are easy to predict and solve with the right joint.

Utility, economy, and the work's aesthetic priorities all influence the choice of joinery for a design. Certain styles seem to exist just to showcase well-crafted joinery, while in others an overall look predominates and assembly techniques are hidden. Elaborate joinery is time-consuming and not always necessary for structure, nor economically justified for function. The wide range of visible and invisible joints can accommodate every taste.

Joinery combined with lumber selection can show wood grain and figure effectively as the focus of a design, as an important element, or reduce an excess of the grain's visual distraction in the overall piece. Economy again tempers aesthetics, as certain cuts waste more wood in the milling process and are more expensive.

Stresses on Joints

Tension *Tension is best overcome by mechanical resistance to the force pulling the joint apart. This can either be an inherent feature of the joint or one added by wedging or pinning.*

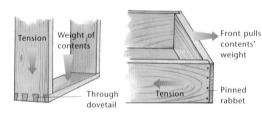

Tension · Weight of contents · Through dovetail

Front pulls contents' weight · Tension · Pinned rabbet

Shear *Shear forces can be a factor when there is insufficient material for loading, but usually shear refers to push/pull stress on a glue line. Such stress can be relieved mechanically by joinery or adding pins, or reinforcing screws.*

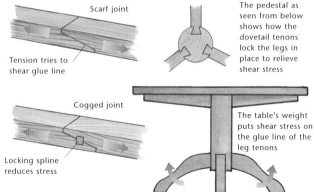

Scarf joint

Tension tries to shear glue line

Cogged joint

Locking spline reduces stress

The pedestal as seen from below shows how the dovetail tenons lock the legs in place to relieve shear stress

The table's weight puts shear stress on the glue line of the leg tenons

Table weight compresses upright and foot

Bending or Racking *The resistance of individual joints to bending can be increased, as can the rigidity against joints bending in unison, which is called racking.*

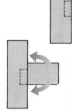

A single-shouldered blind tenon can be made more rigid by adding a second shoulder, dividing the tenon into two, or running a single tenon full depth and wedging it

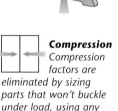

Compression *Compression factors are eliminated by sizing parts that won't buckle under load, using any species dense enough not to compress at the joint line.*

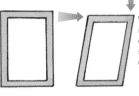

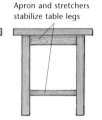

Without reinforcement, open box shape is unstable

A back, bottom or face frame minimizes racking in box structures

Adding or increasing frame structures in a table, such as deeper aprons or stretchers between the legs, will also combat racking.

Apron too narrow to prevent racking

Wider apron stabilizes table legs

Apron and stretchers stabilize table legs

Joinery Style

By hiding or articulating the same basic joint, the "look" of a piece can change dramatically.

A tusked tenon is articulated to emphasize joinery

A blind mortise-and-tenon is blended by sculpting

Joinery and Grain Pattern

Edge joints combined with arrangements of matched lumber yield a variety of visual effects.

How lumber matches are taken from the log

Slip match

Book match

Book matches alternate between top and bottom faces

Slip matches keep the same face always up

Butted   Mitered

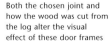

Flatsawn

Quartersawn

Both the chosen joint and how the wood was cut from the log alter the visual effect of these door frames

The waterfall, a length bevel joint cut from one board, continues the grain pattern over an angle

Glues and gluing

Classifying glue by what it is made from (animal, vegetable, or mineral) is not as important as how the glue cures, either by solvent evaporation, chemical reaction, or heat setting. Woodworkers who know these processes can manipulate them to prolong assembly time or speed up drying. When the solvent that is evaporating is water, temporary swelling or warping from introduced moisture can be planned for, avoided, or even encouraged, as would be required for successful biscuit joinery.

Gluing science is complex, but for woodworking it can be reduced to basics. A handful of glues will handle most general needs. Situations for other than a general purpose glue are gluing oily, resinous, or particularly dense woods; gluing for a damp or wet environment; bonding nonporous material like stone or metal to wood; instant bonding for modelmaking or repairs; bent laminating which requires a non-plastic glue that won't flow or stretch under tension; assembly requiring reversibility of the bond for anticipated repairs; or needing a long "open" time for a complicated glue-up.

The aim of gluing is to create a continuous adhesive film between the mating parts and hold them in it until the glue dries and cures enough for safe handling. Some glues don't develop full bond strength for days. The amount of glue to spread, the spreading method, the time open before clamping, the clamping time, the drying time, and the cure time vary by type and brand, so follow the manufacturers' instructions for best results. Soft woods are generally easier to glue than woods whose density makes glue penetration difficult and where over-clamping can squeeze the glue too thin.

Designing Joints

Wood Grain and Bond Strength

End grain glued to any other grain has much reduced bond strength, so butted joints should rely on joinery to create long-grain contact between the parts.

Long grain glued parallel to long grain makes a bond as strong as the wood itself, but cross-gluing it, while strong, creates dimensional conflict.

Gluing creates dimensional conflict

Gluing creates dimensional conflict

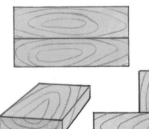

Grain Orientation

Grain orientation in gluing is as important as it is in joint design because the glue bond is strong where there is long-grain to long-grain contact, but weak at any point of end grain contact. Glues help to restrain movement and so contribute to the internal stresses of wood when its moisture content fluctuates. In joints that are glued crossgrain, dimensional conflict and constant wood movement, however minute, stress the glue line. Over time, the combination of tiny constant stresses and the shrinkage of the wood from compression and drying can contribute to an eventual breakdown of the glue bond or material and loosen a joint. Finishing, particularly with films like varnish and polyurethane, can greatly reduce moisture penetration to protect the glue.

Glue Moisture and Joinery

Water-based glues swell the wood at the glue line. If the joint is planed flush before the glue's moisture has dissipated, subsequent moisture loss causes the joint to shrink.

Clamping for Best Bond

All surfaces of a joint should be pulled in snugly, but the direction of clamp pressure is best applied where it enables long-grain contact for the strongest glue bond.

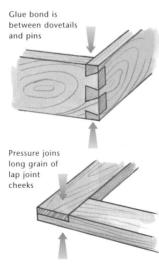

Glue bond is between dovetails and pins

Pressure joins long grain of lap joint cheeks

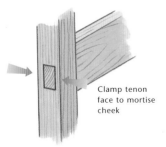

Clamp tenon face to mortise cheek

Wrong Moisture Content If the humidity of a project's final environment differs markedly from that in which it was constructed, joints that fit on assembly could shrink or expand more than the glue or material can withstand. This applies as much to wood assembled in a damp basement and brought to a centrally heated second floor as it does to tropical furniture moved to the desert.

Bad Surface Preparation Modern gluing theory prescribes that cleanly shaven mating surfaces must make full, flat contact for a good glue bond to form. High spots prevent full contact, as do low spots that allow the glue to "pool." The hairiness of a roughsawn surface breaks the glue film. Exotic woods have surface chemicals that require special glues or wiping down with acetone for a good bond.

Glues and Gluing

21

GLUE CHART

	PVA (white glue)	Aliphatic Resin (yellow glue)	Dry Hide Glue	Polyurethane
Wood and wood materials	Yes	Yes	Yes	Yes
Nonporous materials	No	No	Yes	Yes
Preparation or mixing	No	No	Yes	No
Cure method	Solvent evaporation	Solvent evaporation	Solvent evaporation	Moisture catalyzed
Open time	Average	Average	High	Average
Clamp time	Average	Average	None to average	Average
Water-resistant	No	No	No	Yes
Waterproof	No	No	No	Yes
Sandable	No: gums up	Yes	Yes	Yes
Gap-filling	No	No	Yes	No
Reversible/ repairable	Yes	No	Yes	No
Thermoplastic (creeps)	Yes	Yes	No	No
Bonds oily or resinous wood	Yes**	Yes**	Yes**	Yes
Water clean-up	Yes	Yes	Yes	No
Solvent clean-up	No	No	No	Yes
Cost	Low	Low	Low	Moderate
Health/safety concerns	No	No	No	Potential skin sensitivity; fumes

* not for structured bonds   ** with acetone wash   *** water-based type only

Resorcinol Formaldehyde	Urea Formaldehyde (plastic resin)	Epoxy Resin	Cyanoacrylate (superglue)	Contact Cement
Yes	Yes	Yes	Yes	Yes*
No	No	Yes	Yes	Yes
Yes	Yes	Yes	No	No
Catalyzation	Catalyzation	Catalyzation	Moisture catalyzed	Solvent evaporation
High	High	High	Seconds	High
High	High	High	None	None
Yes	Yes	Yes	Yes	Yes
Yes	No	Yes	No	No
Yes: dust toxic	Yes: dust toxic	Yes: difficult	Yes	No
Yes	No	Yes	Yes	No
No	No	No	No	Yes
No	No	No	No	Yes
Yes**	No	Yes	Yes	No
Yes	Yes	No	No	Yes***
No	No	Yes	Yes	Yes
High	Moderate	High	Very High	High
Formaldehyde gas fumes	Formaldehyde gas fumes	Toxic until dry; irritant	Bonds skin; eye irritant	Toxic fumes; flammable

ABOUT EDGE JOINTS

E dge joints are not entirely free from problems of wood movement. However, these problems relate more to the elements of the whole than to the joints themselves. For example, there are a number of considerations for gluing up panels or slabs. When gluing up a slab, whether to place all boards heartwood face up or alternate them up and down is a matter of preference and debate among woodworkers. Greater moisture loss at the end of the boards can cause shrinking, splitting, or joint failure and is overcome by the finish or a "sprung" joint. An assembled panel's ends are automatically hidden in frame-and-panel construction, but on a table or other top, adding an aesthetic or stabilizing lipping at the ends requires careful thought because it introduces cross-grain construction.

The tongue-and-groove adds strength to an edge joint and offers an increased gluing surface.

Wood Movement and Edge Joint Gluing

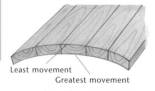

Least movement
Greatest movement

Least movement
Greatest movement

Edge-joined boards with heartwood sides up move as a unit (top), but boards alternating heartwood up and down cup oppositely, making a washboard effect.

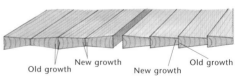

Old growth   New growth   Old growth
New growth

Older growth from the center of the tree and the newer growth of the outer rings shrink and expand differently when edge-joined, creating drawbacks, usually minor in practice.

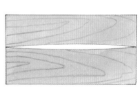

Under clamps, the ¹⁄₃₂" (0.08 cm) hollow of a sprung joint presses ends tightly, anticipating moisture loss so end shrinkage relieves tension on the wood and glue instead of creating it.

Edge and Scarf Joints

Special Jigs for Straightedges and Tapers

Edge clamping doesn't require expensive clamps, but cross clamping requires measures to keep the panel flat, such as alternating clamps top and bottom or using a handscrew or temporary battens at the ends.

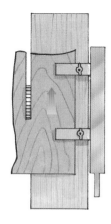

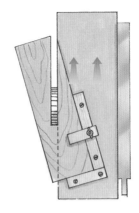

Fasten a crooked board overhanging a sliding plywood carriage to straighten the edge on a table saw.

To taper-cut at the leading end, align the marked taper with a carriage's edge and attach a fence, or notch the carriage to fit the board's outline.

Pinch dogs

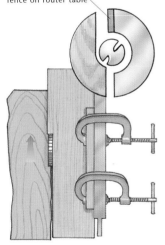

Laminate added to outfeed fence on router table

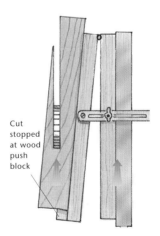

Cut stopped at wood push block

Wedges

Clamps

A fixed jig with an inset equal to the thickness of the saw blade can edge-join a board, as can a router table with a slight fence offset.

An adjustable taper jig has a hinge, a sliding adjuster with wingnut, a handle, and a wood push block for safe cuts to the inside corner.

Use a handscrew to prevent buckling

About Edge Joints

Plain butt glue joint

A butted edge joint is strong enough for the majority of glue-ups for width. It's one of the few edge joints that can be "sprung," or pre-tensioned so later end-grain shrinkage doesn't pull the joint apart. All this joint requires is flat, straight lumber, so the key to success is knowing how to accurately surface and dimension lumber by hand or with power tools.

Edge joints can be handplaned and glued without clamps by rubbing the tacky glue surfaces together. But rubbed joints can't be sprung, for without clamping, edge contact won't occur. Rubbing is suited to lengths under 3' (0.9 m), so a shooting board can be used for edge jointing. It requires glues that quickly develop tack such as animal glues or white or yellow wood glues.

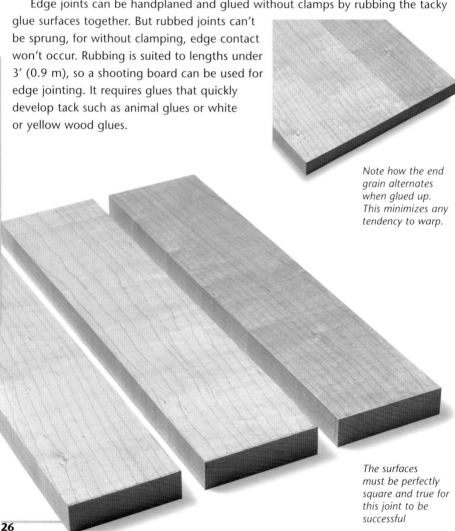

Note how the end grain alternates when glued up. This minimizes any tendency to warp.

The surfaces must be perfectly square and true for this joint to be successful

Plain Butt Glue Joint

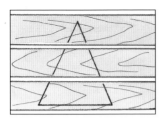

1 Rip stock to within ¼" (0.6 cm) of final width, then cut to length or leave enough for trimming after glue-up. Arrange for grain pattern, and mark for position.

4 Clamp mated edges together and lightly shave just to remove mill marks, or use a short sole to plane in a ¹⁄₃₂" (0.08 cm) hollow for a sprung joint.

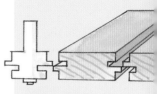

Machined Locking Edge A glue joint cutter used in a router or router table increases the gluing surface and keeps boards aligned during glue-up. Alternatively, use a tongue-and-groove joint (see page 31), a shiplap joint (see page 30), or a splined joint (see page 29) to achieve the same effect.

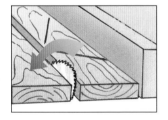

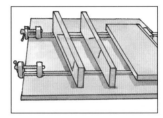

2 After rough ripping, trim each edge to final dimensions, alternating mating boards up and down to cancel any out-of-square in the blade setting.

5 Set out the clamps on a flat surface and assemble the boards, checking for fit; then stand boards on edge to spread glue, and clamp with battens protecting the edges.

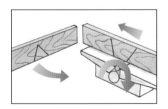

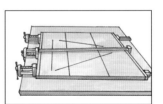

3 For final dimensioning on the jointer, always feed stock to cut with the grain to avoid tear-out. Don't alternate faces to cancel out-of-square; set a precise fence to allow jointing for best grain direction.

6 Align the threaded screw with the board edge and counteract bowing with clamps on both sides; tighten the clamps alternately so the assembly doesn't pop apart, then let the glue dry and trim the ends square.

Handplaned Rubbed Joint

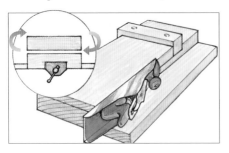

1 Shoot edges and test straightness, rotating one board against the other in the vise to find crowning that will rock the board, or hollowing that causes ends to scrape.

2 Check edges for squareness and correct any small deviation by steadying the plane with a knuckle against the board and planing the high spot until a full shaving can be taken along the length.

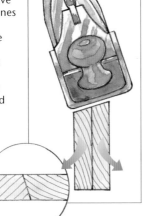

3 An alternative method planes both edges together in the vise so when aligned flat, as shown, any deviation from 90° is cancelled by the mating edge.

4 Whatever the method used for jointing the edges, a straightedge will lie flat across the joint if the technique is successful.

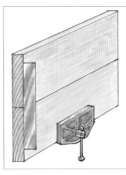

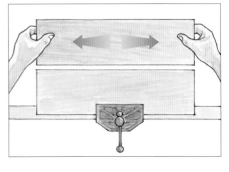

5 Lay thin stock flat for rubbing, or clamp thicker stock in the vise, holding the top board low down to slide back and forth in the glue until suction grabs it.

6 Joints in thin wood shouldn't be disturbed until dry, but when it's safe to move the boards from the vise, lean them against a support until they dry thoroughly.

Splined joint

Splining is a quick and easy way to reinforce an edge joint. If referenced from the marked face, it takes little calculation or layout for an accurate joint with perfect alignment of the faces. Splining also prevents slippage until the glue has dried. Man-made materials work well for splines. Exactly-sized masonite is the easiest to match to standard cutter widths. Less accurate plywood might require two grooving passes with an undersized cutter for a good fit. Splines cut from solid wood are limited in length by the board's width, and it takes several splines to equal the single continuous length possible from man-made materials where grain direction is not an issue. Be sure to test for fit in a test groove.

By use of a contrasting material, an attractive detail can be incorporated.

Spline

Grooves

Splined Joint

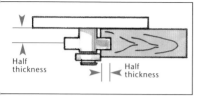

Half thickness

Half thickness

1 With a router registering from the marked face of each board, run a groove in the center of each edge to a depth of about half the wood thickness.

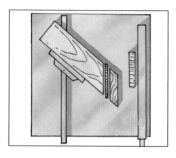

2 Match spline material thickness to the groove width of about one third to half the stock thickness; rip cross-grain strips just under double the grooving depth.

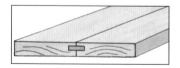

3 Test for fit: splines too wide prevent closing; tight ones could stress the groove when swollen by glue moisture. Spread glue on lips and along grooves, assemble, and clamp.

Edge and Scarf Joints

VARIATIONS

Capped Spline When the joint runs through and shows on the finished piece, a capped spline improves the appearance of a plywood spline or creates an effect with matching or contrasting wood.

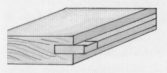

Stopped Spline A stopped spline keeps the joinery hidden, or holds the spline back so further work like shaping the edge doesn't expose it.

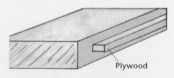

Plywood

Shiplap A shiplap is two mated rabbets that help alignment and increase the gluing surface. The rabbet depth should be half the thickness of the stock.

Each board of the shiplap must be wide enough to include the rabbet depth. Routed, shaped, or cut with a dado, the joint exposes additional long-grain gluing surface in a rabbet. It also serves to align the faces flush. In bowed lumber, this advantage is cancelled unless there is downward clamping at the center of the boards, which is difficult to accomplish in a large slab glue-up.

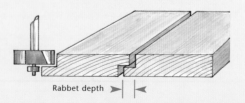

Rabbet depth

Tongue and groove

The tongue is like an integral spline that reinforces and aligns the joint but takes a little more calculation to machine. Boards must be ripped wider to provide material for the tongue. Even without special grooving tools or a dado head, the table saw makes an acceptable joint with a combination or rip blade that has a raker, a square tooth that leaves the bottom of the kerf flat. Bowed lumber will misalign the groove or make the tongue uneven unless hold-downs and fingerboards are used to keep the lumber against the fence. Add a high wood fence for stability or to prevent cutters from contacting the metal fence.

The tongue-and-groove has been used for good-quality flooring and wainscot paneling for centuries.

Tongue

Groove

Tongue and Groove

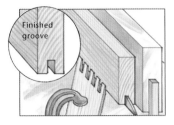

Finished groove

1 Raise a raker-toothed blade to half the stock thickness, set the fence to one third the thickness from the blade, make one grooving pass, and reverse the board so the second pass widens the groove.

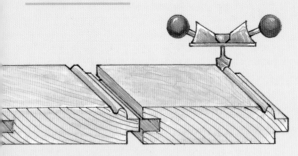

Tongue and Bead Adding a bead to the edge of a tongue-and-groove joint in assembled panels in furniture adds visual interest and enables a dry-fitting option for handling wood movement over an otherwise difficult expanse.

The tongue-and-bead, commonly seen in wainscotting, is easily added to a tongue-and-groove joint with a router, moulding plane, or scratch beader.

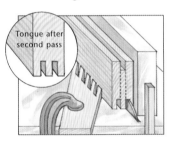

Tongue after second pass

2 Lower the blade a hair so the tongue is not too long, move the fence in to shave the tongue just outside the width of the groove, and reverse for the second pass.

V-Groove Edges without tongues most often appear on vertical surfaces because of their tendency to catch debris. The V-groove or any similar detail accentuates the joint. It is easy to cut before glue-up but hard to keep free of glue squeeze-out. The table saw set at 45°, or a plane or router can cut chamfers to form V-grooves for a paneling detail.

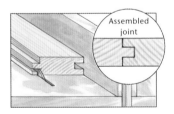

Assembled joint

3 Test that the tongue fits the groove. Lower the blade and set the fence to cut the waste from the shoulders at the tongue's depth, fitting the joint as shown.

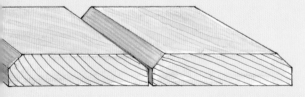

ABOUT SCARF JOINTS

The shallow angle of the basic glued scarf (or splice) joint exposes long-grain surfaces for a good glue joint. Simple gluing at the slope ratio of 1:8 bonds the parts into a unit that theory says is as strong as a single board. Like edge joints, there is no perfect solution to orienting the growth rings of solid wood scarfed parts—either to cup opposite to each other or to cup in the same direction. Worked scarfs that are more than simple glue joints also expose long grain for gluing, but in imitation of their timber-framing ancestors, employ fitted joinery, locking, and pinning to hold the joint together. When scarfs are used structurally, another member should give direct or nearby support and, if needed, provide a place to hide a less than decorative joint. Used visually as a design element, elaborate scarf joints that defy machining are the most challenging and awe-inspiring of all woodworking joints.

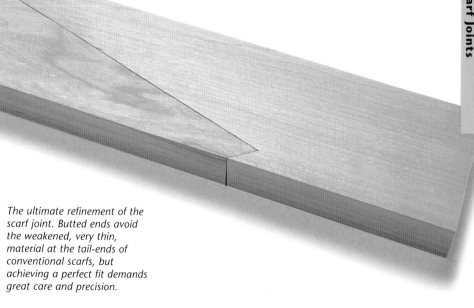

The ultimate refinement of the scarf joint. Butted ends avoid the weakened, very thin, material at the tail-ends of conventional scarfs, but achieving a perfect fit demands great care and precision.

End-to-end scarf

Gluing boards end to end doesn't make a pretty joint, but it is very practical. For extreme strength in a glue-only joint, use epoxy. With any glue, first spread a priming coat that will wick up into the grain, filling the hollow cells so the next coat stays at the gluing surface.

This scarf can be made angled, as when it is used to angle a guitar's peg head back from the neck: both parts are aligned bevel side up, and one bevel is glued to the back of the other bevel, creating the angle. Draw the parts of a desired angle full-size in profile to find the angle setting for the sliding bevel to use in laying out the parts.

The end-to-end scarf is useful for extending the length of skirting boards, dado rails, and architraves.

End-to-End Scarf

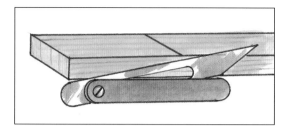

1 Measure from each board end to eight times
its thickness, square a line across the face, set
the sliding bevel to the 1:8 angle and mark it on
both edges.

2 If width prevents
wasting the acute
bevel with any saw and
planing smooth, start at
the top corner and plane
the entire bevel back to
the squared line. Skew
the plane to prevent
break-out.

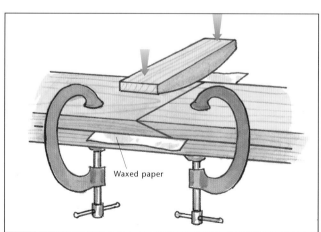

Waxed paper

3 Using waxed paper where glue may ooze, immobilize the
parts against slipping and clamp the joint or, on a wide joint,
use a crowned batten for pressure in the center.

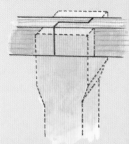

Hidden Lines The
unsightly joint line
of a half-lapped or
other light-duty
scarf used to
extend an apron
can be supported
and hidden inside
a table leg.

Angled Faces
Angling the joining
faces of any scarf
increases resistance
to bending and
shear, but layout
lines must be
exactly scribed
with a knife, sawn
slightly oversize,
and shaved clean
for a tight fit.

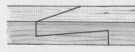

End-to-End Scarf

Edge-to-edge scarf

Edge-to-edge scarf is a utilitarian joint that joins lumber for increased length. It can be used to stretch out a too-short board by first ripping it diagonally, then sliding the halves a little along the cutting angle, gluing, and finally trimming to width when dry. A spline can reduce the extreme angle required for a glue-only joint by introducing mechanical reinforcement and another gluing surface. Gluing is best preceded by a priming coat to prevent a glue-starved joint.

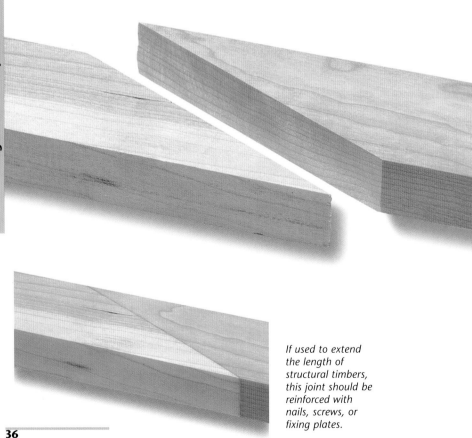

If used to extend the length of structural timbers, this joint should be reinforced with nails, screws, or fixing plates.

Edge-to-Edge Scarf

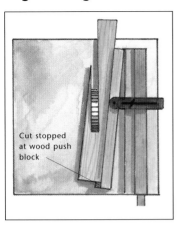

1 For a strong glue joint, make a taper eight times the board's width, or set the jig to cut any angle under 20° for nonstructural work if the species glues well.

Cut stopped at wood push block

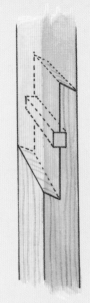

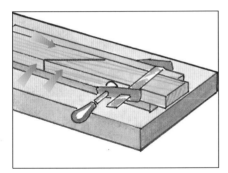

2 Apply glue and clamp one part to the fence of a nonstick gluing sled, press the mate in against it and clamp both to the fence until the joint dries.

Adding Keys
Angled ends resist bending, and inserting a transverse key into two aligning dadoes kerfed across a lowered sawblade additionally fortifies a joint against tension and shearing.

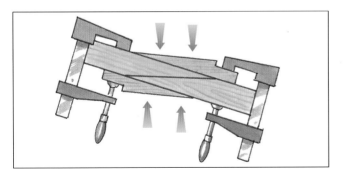

3 Alternatively, clamp the notched cutoffs to the parts, creating a parallel purchase for clamping the joint. Stop slipping by using a biscuit, or a doweled headless brad pressed between the parts.

Squint-butted scarf

The squint-butted scarf is a simple start on worked scarfs. Resistant to bending, easy to reinforce and dress up with a transverse key, it has good long-grain contact for gluing. There is no set formula for the length of the lapping surface in worked scarfs. The joinery improves stress resistance or, in some designs, yields true parallel-grain gluing for strength instead of the oblique grain in glue-only joints. But scarf strength depends on the length of the scarf, so knowledge of the principles, an eye for aesthetics, and the application are the best guides. Regardless, layouts should be knife-scribed for exactness. Areas wasted with a saw should be cleaned up with a shoulder plane or chiseled down to the scribed line.

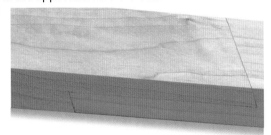

The squint-butted scarf is a difficult joint to execute, but it incorporates a locking key that awards greater strength than a standard end-to-end scarf joint.

Squint-Butted Scarf

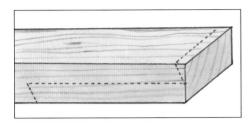

1 Exactly scribe the edge's center line four or more times as long as the board thickness. To this line's ends, scribe from each face parallel lines at 70°.

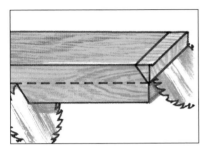

2 Set the saw blade to 70° and cut both parts together if possible, using the miter gauge to trim the ends, then lower the blade and kerf the parts to the center line.

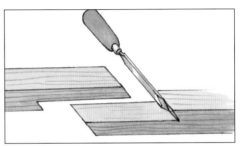

3 Use a handsaw, bandsaw, or table saw to cut the waste along the center line, then guide a chisel against the shoulder to trim inside the corner and slide the joint together.

About lap joints

The halving cuts that form lap joints are basically dadoes or rabbets, although wide dadoes are sometimes called trenches and deep dadoes are often termed notches. A halving cut in the board face results in a frame lap, used in supporting frameworks or framing panels. Edge laps notch into board edges to half the part's width and appear in crossed stretchers, sash mouldings, shoji, chair back, or window lattice, and egg-crate dividers. The large gluing area of a frame lap is long-grain for a strong gluing but always with dimensional conflict. The edge lap has little long-grain contact and the wood, weakened by notching into the width, is liable to split without reinforcement.

A frame lap joint in the T orientation is a simple combination of two basic elements.

Edge laps are light-duty or worked in plywood, whose alternated grains strengthen the material. Frame laps come in two basic versions: end laps are halving rabbets cut at the board's end; center laps are halving dadoes cut somewhere in the board's length. End laps and center laps (rabbets and dadoes) in different combinations form all the basic corner L, T, and crossed-frame lap orientations.

Lapped and Housed Joints

Milled Elements

Rabbet

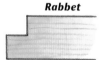

Dado

Notch

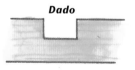

The three basic cuts used to make halvings or lap joints.

Lap Joint Components

An end lap has a single shoulder and is formed by a deep rabbet cut to half the thickness of the stock.

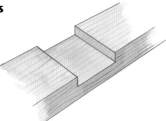

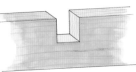

A deep dado notched into the edge of a board forms one half of an edge lap or edge halving joint.

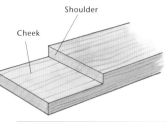

Shoulder

Cheek

A double-shouldered center lap has a dado or trench cut into the face of the board anywhere inside its length.

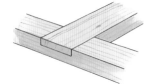

Types of Lap Joint

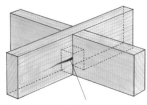

Weak area

Halvings cut into the face of the board and assembled in L, T, or crossed configurations are called frame laps, with excellent gluing strength and shoulders that resist bending.

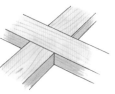

A halving in the edge of the board is called an edge lap, but there is material weakness and no glue strength where unsupported end grain butts to the mating part.

Combining the Elements of Lap Joints

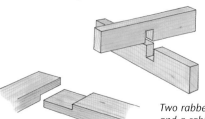

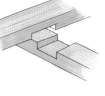

Two rabbets, two dadoes, or a dado and a rabbet are the basic components of all lap joints.

Using Lap Joints

   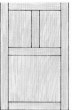 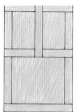

Straight and angled laps are good joints for decorative latticework in windows, doors, outdoor furniture, and structures like gazebos.

It's possible to join a traditional-style door entirely with lap joints that are nearly as strong as a mortise and tenon, but the front and back won't have the same visual lines.

Lapped and Housed Joints

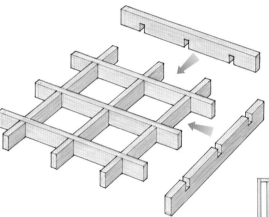

Make egg-crate dividers on the table saw with a notching jig, or saw down by hand and chop out the waste at the bottom of the cut with a chisel.

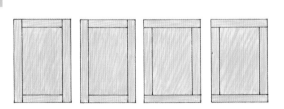

On doors where one side is prominent, lap different pairs of parts on top to shift the design emphasis from a vertical to a horizontal line.

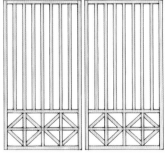

The latticework of traditional Japanese shoji screens is joined by straight and angled lap joints, usually sawn by hand simultaneously in softwood; the mating parts are clamped together.

Shop-made aids to making lap joints

Jigs for Handheld Tools

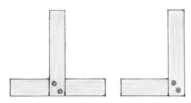

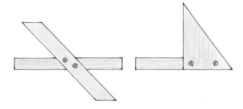

A smooth, straightedge to guide tools squarely across the workpiece is a basic shop accessory that is especially useful when making lap joints.

Angled fences to guide cuts by router, plane, or saw are cheap and easy to make using a protractor head, sliding bevel, and full-sized shop drawing in order to set the angle.

Routing Methods

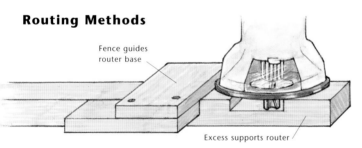

Fence guides router base

Excess supports router

A shop-made square fence guides a router base to make an end lap. Excess end material supports the router and is cut off later.

To rout multiples of dadoes or notches, the workpiece slides under a fence that guides an over-bearing straight bit and is stopped at the shoulder mark by a block that also supports the router.

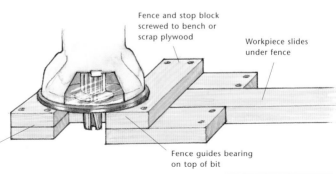

Fence and stop block screwed to bench or scrap plywood

Workpiece slides under fence

Stop block supports router and sets distance to shoulder

Fence guides bearing on top of bit

Jigs for Table Saws and Router Tables

Two basic sliding jigs—an adjustable one for a miter gauge slot and one straddling a moveable fence—support parts vertically so end lap cheeks can be sawn or routed.

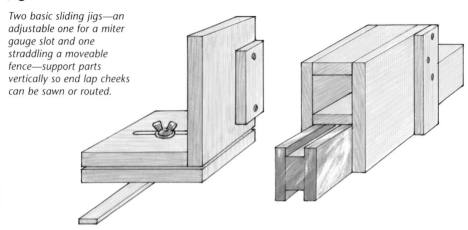

Jigs for Miter Gauge

Two jigs assist repetition of edge notches: one rides miter gauge slots and has an adjustable fence, the other attaches to the miter gauge (see Box Joint on the Table Saw on page 55).

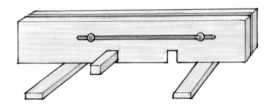

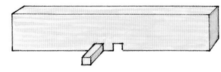

Gluing Lap Joints

For a good glue bond, always use a block under the clamp head to distribute pressure so the long-grain surfaces make full contact.

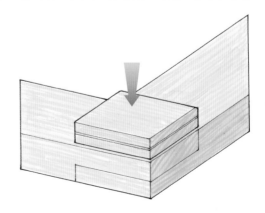

End lap

One end lap can combine with another end lap to form an L-corner lap or it can set into a center lap to make a T-lap joint. One of the safest methods to align a cut is by clamping a spacer block to the saw fence in front of the blade (as shown with the tablesawn end lap on page 46). The part should clear the block before the cut is completed, and better, before it starts. Cheeks and shoulders can be cut by router, and a router table is a handy assistant. If many parts are needed, set up a jig to assist in repetitive cutting and to avoid tedious clamping and unclamping of fences. If the joint is likely to be subjected to lateral force, drilled and countersunk screws will provide additional strength.

Cheek

The end lap is a simple framing joint that is extremely quick to construct but it should not be subjected to any lateral force.

Shoulder

End Lap on the Table Saw

Gluing You can use a lap joint to add gluing strength to the always weak end-grain miter. But because of their substantial long-grain gluing surface, unless they need to resist considerable tension, just gluing laps is usually strong enough.

Miters A mitered halving changes the appearance of an end lap to suit design, but also reduces the gluing surface and consequently the joint strength.

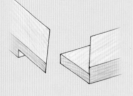

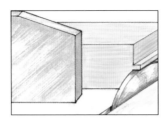

1 Graze a scrap end of the stock with a lowered saw blade, flipping the stock with each subsequent cut and slowly raising the blade until it removes the lip at the center.

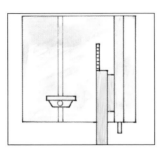

2 Place the stock and a scrap block against the fence and slide the entire assembly over until the edge of the stock aligns with the outer tooth of the blade.

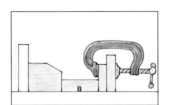

3 Lock the fence and clamp the scrap in front of the blade. Butt the stock against the block and push the cut through with the gauge.

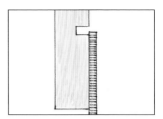

4 After the shoulders are cut on all the parts, raise the blade height into the kerf but making sure it doesn't nick the new shoulder.

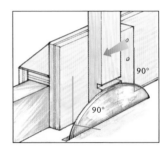

5 Support the stock at 90° to the table and move the fence in until the blade aligns to the depth of the shoulder kerf and clears any screws.

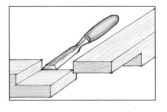

6 After wasting the cheeks using the jig, clean up the inside corner with a chisel if the blade leaves a tiny ridge there, and assemble the joint.

Bandsawn End Lap

Square a shoulder line at stock width, mark an edge center line, kerf into the waste near the shoulder, and set a stop block at cutting depth to waste the cheek.

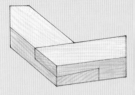

Cutting Cheeks

Tilt the saw blade slightly and stop-cut one cheek end first, shaving the other part's cheek held upright of this will fortify a weight bearing framing lap, like one for a glass door.

Routed End Lap

1 Fit the router table with a straight bit and bump-cut the edge of some scrap stock. Flip and cut again, raising the bit until the cuts center.

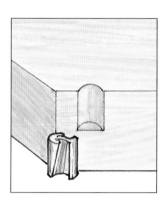

2 With a square of grip-cleated scrap plywood to steady it, clean the joint by feeding the part back and forth across the bit while at the same time sliding it toward the fence.

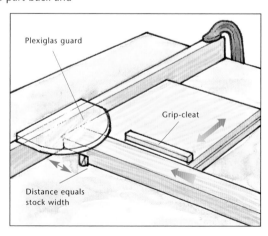

Plexiglas guard

Grip-cleat

Distance equals stock width

Dovetail Laps

Halve a single dovetail and scribe its angled shoulder on the back of the mating part as another way to reinforce against tension on the glue line

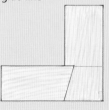

Center lap

There are many methods for removing the waste between the shoulders of a center lap. Sawing repetitive kerfs to just short of half the part's thickness, either by hand or machine, weakens the material so it can be broken out and the cheek cleaned up by chiseling, hand planing, or routing. Another way is to rout out the cheek material with a handheld router, or remove it using a router table aided by a miter gauge or sliding jig to steady the part. Possibly no other joint requires as much material removal as a halving joint. A dado head cutter removes material quite effectively, but some types don't leave an entirely flat bottom, or the outer teeth leave deeper scribe marks that will show at the glue line. Wasting cuts have to be held short of the center line and cleaned up by hand tools or a router.

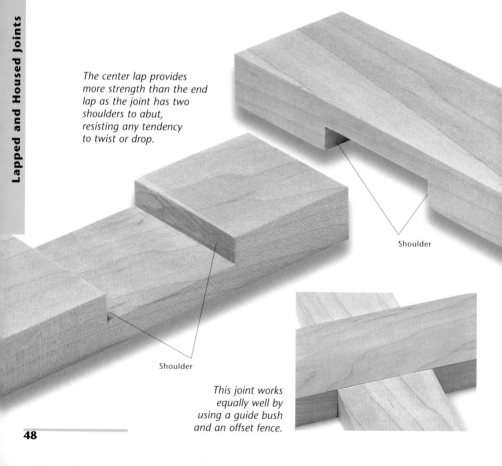

The center lap provides more strength than the end lap as the joint has two shoulders to abut, resisting any tendency to twist or drop.

Shoulder

Shoulder

This joint works equally well by using a guide bush and an offset fence.

Center Lap by Hand

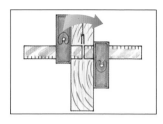

1 Scribe a line near the end grain's center, flip the square and scribe again, split the marks and set the blade to the exact center, then scribe the end and joint's edge.

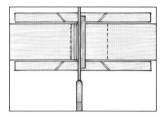

4 Lay out the shoulders as far apart as the width of the stock to be joined, and square them across to make a series of saw cuts between them in the waste.

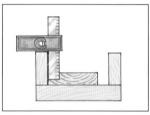

2 Put the stock, blocked up if necessary, in a miter box and extend and lock the square's blade, keeping it just shy of the center mark on the end of the stock.

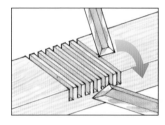

5 Break away the waste with a chisel and carefully pare the ridges left at the bottom of the joint plus any saw marks left on the shoulders.

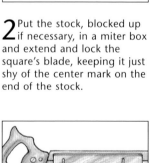

3 Use the setting to adjust a depth stop on the saw, covering the square's beam temporarily with masking tape or taking care not to scrape the saw's teeth on it.

6 If possible, use a bullnose, shoulder, or rabbet plane to square the shoulders and flatten the bottom level with the edge center line for the best glue surface.

Center Laps A fully housed center lap is often a face-frame joint for built-ins where the end grain won't show, or just a stabilizing rail. But without a shoulder on the housed part, the rack resistance isn't as good as with two halved and shouldered parts. A joint that is halved and lapped with a dovetailed end like the dovetailed center or T-lap has high tension and rack resistance and is an excellent contributor to solid framed structures. It also would be useful as a stabilizing center stile in a structure like shelving with lipped edges.

Center Lap

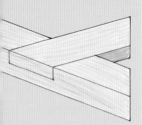

Full Lap A full lap houses one part's thickness in another part's face; a face housing sets the full part into an edge, making joints especially useful when the thinner part continues past.

Dovetails Cut a single or double dovetail on an end lap and scribe around it to mark the center lap shoulders for strengthening a T-lap against tension.

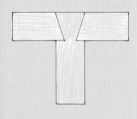

Routed Center Lap

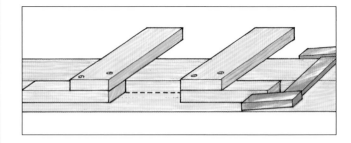

1 Scribe the joint's center line and shoulders, align some square shop-made router guides across the stock on the shoulder lines, and clamp them there.

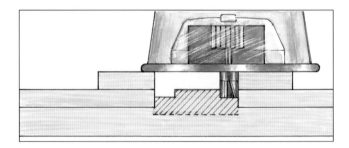

2 Guiding a router and top-bearing straight bit from left to right against the guides, make shallow passes that cut the shoulders, then waste the material between them.

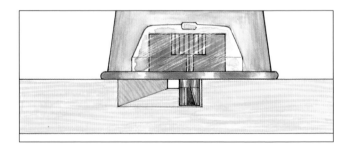

3 If a short bit can't reach the center line, remove the guides and use the new shoulders as guides for the bearing, continuing shallow passes to reach the joint's bottom.

Angled T-lap

It's very easy to cut the angle of the center lap tilted in the wrong direction if careful attention isn't paid. The radial-arm saw is only one method for milling this joint. It's simple to rout handheld using an angled fence. The table saw also will cut the cheeks of the T-shaped part, aided by a sliding fence jig. Since the ends of the T-shaped part aren't square but angled, the support block on the jig has to be tilted away from the blade to the angle that holds the end of the mitered T-shaped part flat against the table.

Use the table saw miter gauge to steady the work for repeated kerfs across the center lap to waste the material between the shoulders. A dadoing head will waste the center lap material, but watch out for it lifting the part off the table.

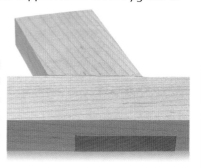

Take care in setting out this joint and you will be rewarded with an attractive and strong joint.

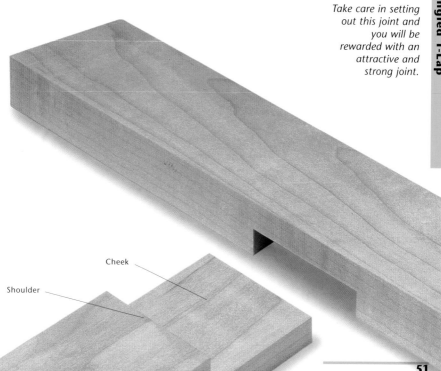

Cheek

Shoulder

Angled T-Lap on the Radial-Arm Saw

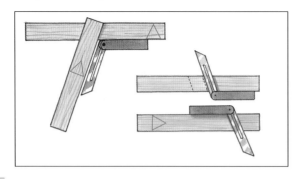

1 Mark the angled shoulder position on the faces of the parts, squaring it around to the back of the center-lap part and scribing it by using the bevel gauge setting.

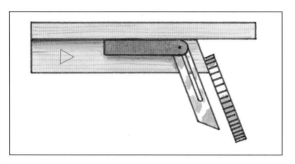

2 Use the same angle to set the radial-arm sawblade and cut the T-shaped part to length.

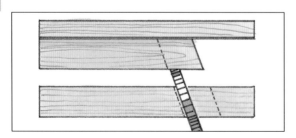

3 Raise the blade to the center line of the stock thickness and kerf across at the shoulder lines, then waste the center-lap material with a series of kerfs that run across it.

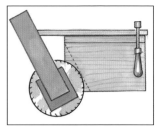

4 Turn the blade to the horizontal position and clamp a height table for clearance to the saw fence. Mark the cutting path of the blade's outer diameter on it.

5 Raise the blade to cut into the cheek waste at the center line. Pull the cut through, so that the shoulder doesn't move beyond the marked blade path.

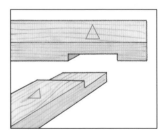

6 Clean up the cheeks with a chisel or shoulder plane, turn the center-lap part face up and assemble.

Jigged edge lap

The edge notching jig is useful if more than a couple of notches and parts are being cut. The jig works on the table saw or router table, but with either machine, tear-out at the back of the workpiece where the cutter passes through is more than difficult to control, especially in soft or coarse-grained woods. A scrap backing board between the workpiece and fence will help, or cut all the notches to width in overthick stock and make clean-up passes by handplane, planer, or saw in order to thickness the parts to fit the notches.

The lack of glue strength on the end grain of this joint can cause problems.

VARIATIONS

Angled and Edge Lap Variations To find the angles for an angled cross lap, draw a square on paper, or start from a corner of a sheet of plywood to lay out the actual height and width of the "X" and take the crossing angles from it with an architect's triangle or sliding T-bevel. Pin through the joint with dowels or plugged screws for extra reinforcement. Another way to add strength is to increase the shoulder proportion as in the shouldered angled lap.

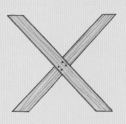

Angled Cross The angled cross lap, reinforceable with pins, gives good support to casual tables while the angled edge lap allows stretchers between table and chair legs to run diagonally.

Narrow Angled Lap Decreasing the width of the angled lap strengthens the center-lap member by removing less wood while fortifying the shoulder base against racking.

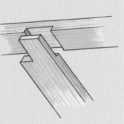

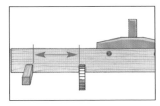

Using Dadoes Reinforcing an edge lap against twisting by housing the thickness of one member in secondary dadoes has the effect of relating the edge lap to the bridle joint family (see Mortise-and-Tenon Joints, page 68).

Jigged Edge Lap

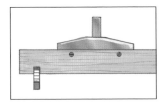

1 Match the stock thickness to a router bit or dado cutter mounted in a table saw and use a miter gauge to notch a scrap half the stock width deep.

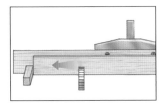

2 Fit an indexing key to the notch, clamp the scrap to the miter gauge, cut a second notch at the desired spacing, screw the scrap to the gauge, and unclamp.

3 Butt the stock to the index key to cut the first notch. Fit the first notch over the index and cut again, advancing the stock for each new notch.

Box joint on the table saw

T he box joint, also called the fingerlap or comb joint, is a design spawned by machinery. Aesthetically, the proportions of fingers and notches look best if they are as wide as the stock thickness, half the stock thickness or the thickness of a saw blade kerf. If a friction fit is achieved, the exceptional amount of long-grain glue surface between the fingers makes the fingerlap the dovetail's rival for strength.

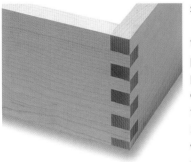

This joint is also known as a comb joint and is used primarily in industrial furniture construction. It is almost as strong as a dovetail but is far easier to set out.

As with the edge lap and its jig, machining the box joint on the table saw presents the problem of tear-out. The box joint notch parallels the grain instead of crossing it as it does in the edge lap, so the tear-out is only at the top of the notch, not at both sides. Scribing a line across the board where the top will fall is the method recommended to prevent tear-out.

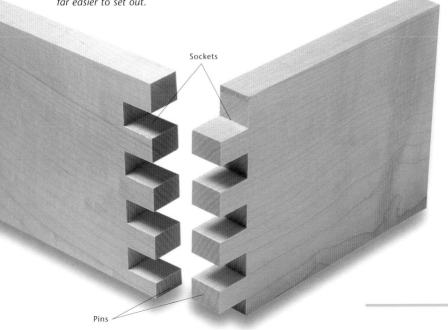

Sockets

Pins

Making a Box Joint on the Table Saw

Box Joint Variations

The decorative effect of box joints is a starting point for alterations and applications that draw attention to the interlocking pattern of the fingers. One famous woodworker has used the hinging option to attach drop leaves at the ends of his tabletops. He staggers the ends of the glued-up boards in the top to create fingers and notches, then fits in and pins an alternately staggered leaf.

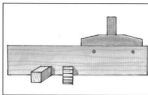

1 Make a jig like the edge lap jig for the miter gauge, but match the key, notch, and spacing to the dado's width, and set the notch height just under the stock thickness.

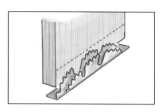

4 Set the dado height to the scribed line to leave the fingers protruding for sanding flush after assembly, the stock being cut to slightly over the final length.

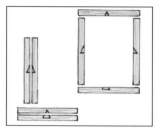

2 Choose the outside faces and mark the parts to distinguish sides from fronts and backs, and to show the reference edge to be used against the indexing key.

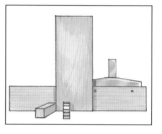

5 Butt a side's reference edge against the key with scribed face toward the jig, cut a notch, then check that the new notch and finger are exactly the same width.

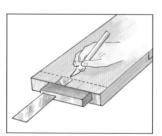

3 With the reference edge close and the end always at the left hand, scribe across each end at a setting just over the stock thickness.

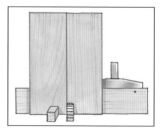

6 Reverse the side and index it over the key, then butt a front or back against it with the scribed line in to cut a notch at its reference edge.

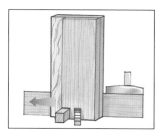

7 To gang the dadoing, turn the side back around and index it over the key, butt up the back's half notch, and advance the parts together to cut additional notches.

Deep Variations Cutting notches deeper than the stock thickness lets the fingers of a box joint stand proud for a decorative effect that is additionally enhanced by chamfering around each finger's end.

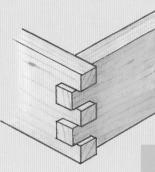

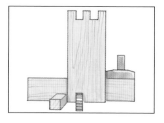

8 Keeping the reference edges toward the key, turn the boards end for end and repeat, making sure to start each part with a finger or notch like its other end.

Rounded corners After a box joint is glued, round the corner by hand or with a router for a bricklaid appearance that is friendly to the touch.

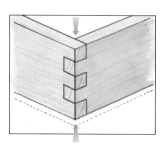

9 Trim any bottom waste edge to width. A wider or narrower last finger will fall there and glue together so clamping pressure seats the fingers for long-grain contact.

Hinged Joints Dry-assemble the fingers and drill through their centers, round the end, and then insert a waxed dowel or brass pin to make a wood hinge for joining to a box lid.

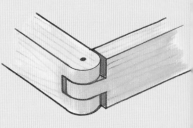

ABOUT HOUSED JOINTS

Although they are made from the same basic cuts as lap joints, instead of the equal partnership of lap joints, housed joints have an implied hierarchy because one part *houses* the other. In joint terminology, there's a difference between the hous*er* and the hous*ee*. When a cabinet back is set into a rabbet, the joint is called a rabbet housing. If the rabbet itself is housed, it's a housed rabbet. But the basic housing cut (the houser) is always a dado, rabbet, or groove.

A joint is a full housing when it fully encloses one part (the housee) in the U shape of a dado or groove, or the "step" of a rabbet. A partial housing encloses some of the part, usually a tongue, while one or two shoulders bear on the face of the wood into which the housing is cut to stabilize the joint.

Even if shoulders improve on the full housing's lack of racking resistance, housed joints are not very strong. Aside from having no mechanical resistance to tension unless they are modified, in most T orientations with dado housing like shelving and some L orientations with rabbet housings, there is no long-grain gluing contact. But the shear resistance of the joint used for shelving is suited to the purpose, and cabinet backs add stability.

Dovetails are used to modify the tongues of housed parts and the housings themselves to increase tension resistance in housed joints. Variations include housing joints and sliding dovetail joints (see Dovetail joints on page 130).

The most common housed joints are the ones used to join fixed shelving into place, but housings also hold drawer runners and drawer frames inside carcasses, let cabinet backs be set in, or like the pinned rabbet housing shown in Full-housed Variations, page 61, serve as the drawer corner joint of Japanese woodworking. Housings modified by dovetails mechanically prevent racking or restraint bowing as cross-members in framed structures like table aprons, and as shelf joints resist forces pushing tall cabinet sides outward.

Shop made Aids to Making Housed Joints

A T-square fence guides dadoes by a router if it's run along the fence into the beam, cutting the dado width and location to align the fence and layout.

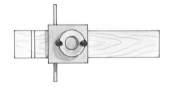

An auxiliary router base with fixed runner matching the cutter's width will cut equidistant dadoes.

Attach a depth stop through holes drilled slowly into a tenon saw to avoid losing blade temper, or use small spring or C-clamps to hold the stop on.

The Elements of Housings

A full dado housing encloses the thickness of the joining part. Both parts move as a unit across their widths, but the glue surface is end grain.

A full-rabbet housing has no glue strength and no resistance to tension.

Increasing tension resistance means using other elements to create a suitable joint, here a full-housed lap dovetail.

Whether it's full or partial, a through housing will show the intersection of the parts at the face.

A full-grooved housing runs with the grain, and the housed part's grain is run parallel so there is no dimensional conflict and the glue bond is excellent.

A stopped housing is held short of the part's edge (below) and the joining member is notched back slightly at the face to hide the joinery.

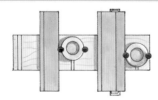

Another fence will space equidistant dadoes by router, but an additional spacer strip can be inserted to increase the height between shelves.

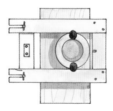

A saddle jig fits over the workpiece. The sides guide the router across it from the end entry hole to cut through or be stopped by a block.

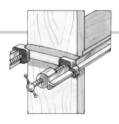

To transfer clamp pressure to the center of long dadoes, cut slightly crowned cauls for each shelf end and tighten a bar clamp parallel to each edge.

Full housing by hand

A full housing has little resistance to racking and less to tension, so consider the overall structure before choosing this joint. A tapped-home fit makes the joint work mechanically and aesthetically, but it is a fit that is easily lost to sanding of the housed part. With no shoulder to cover any deviations along the dado edge, accuracy and the flatness of the housed part are both in sharp focus.

A housing deeper than half the thickness of the part will weaken it; a depth one third the thickness is all that's necessary. If you are housing drawer runners in solid wood so cross-grain construction is introduced, screw the runners at the front of the carcass and slot-screw them at the back without glue to allow for wood movement.

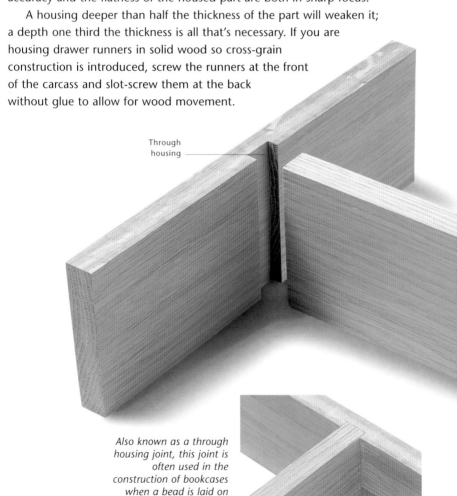

Through housing

Also known as a through housing joint, this joint is often used in the construction of bookcases when a bead is laid on the front edge to conceal the joint.

Full Housing by Hand

1 Mark one shoulder of each dado on the board's face, planning waste to fall on the same side of the marks, then transfer the layout to the mating parts.

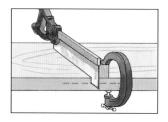

4 Guiding the saw against the block and into the chiseled bevel, cut across the board until the saw reaches the dado depth when its back hits the stop block.

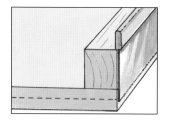

2 Cut a block whose height added to the dado depth will equal the sawblade measured from teeth to back.

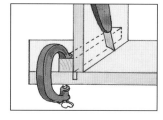

5 Use the thickness of the stock to be housed as a gauge to score a line for the other shoulder of the dado.

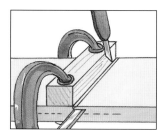

3 Clamp the block square across the stock at the mark, score the board along the block, then chisel a small guide bevel in the waste side.

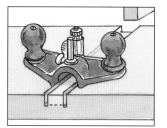

6 Align the block on the second score and repeat the sawing process, then chisel or router plane to a flat bottom and fit the shelf.

Full-Housed Variations

Increasing the full housing's resistance to tension isn't hard, but frequently it means borrowing from the dovetail family. The mortise-and-tenon joint shown on page 76 is a quick and easy strengthening modification. At the front few inches of the dado, the dado's square U shape is stopped and a narrower dovetail housing is cut. A short section of the shelf end is shaped to match, and the joint slides home from the back. If the grain of the parts runs vertically, a full rabbet housing makes a strong glue joint. But a full rabbet housing at a corner with only end-grain contact won't hold together under tension unless it's reinforced. Pinning is one good cure that makes a quick but strong drawer corner joint.

Full housing on the table saw

For aesthetic reasons, the housing is sometimes stopped back from the front edge. The front corner of the shelf that would be housed in a through dado is cut off, notching in a small shoulder that bears on the material left in front of the dado by stopping it. A stopped cut on a table saw is difficult and dangerous, especially one running across the grain, and the stopped kerf of the blade leaves an arc to square up. Removing a thin strip from the front edge before dadoing and regluing it later resolves the mechanical and aesthetic problems of dadoing on the table saw.

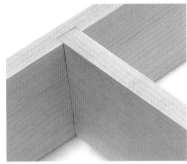

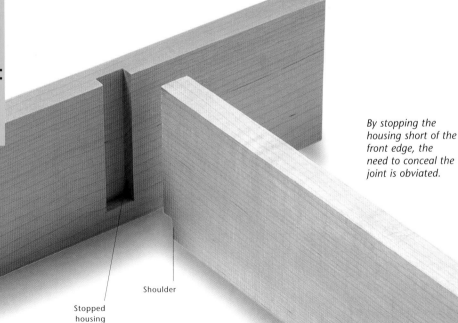

By stopping the housing short of the front edge, the need to conceal the joint is obviated.

Shoulder

Stopped housing

Full Housing on the Table Saw

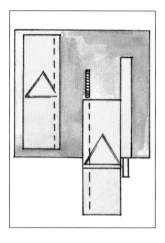

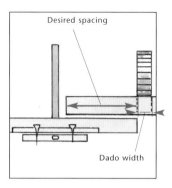

Desired spacing

Dado width

1 Mark the dado parts for reassembly. Rip and save narrow strips from their front edges so each part equals the desired width when the strips are reglued later.

2 Screw a scrap fence to the miter gauge and trim its end with a dado cutter matched to shelf thickness. Dado another scrap at the desired depth and spacing.

Short Dovetails A short dovetailed section at the front of a full housing strengthens the joint against tension but avoids the problems of a full sliding dovetail.

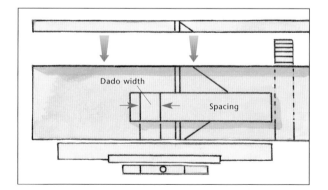

Dado width

Spacing

Stopped Dadoes To make a stopped dado by hand, first drill a flat-bottomed hole to dado depth at the front, squaring it with a chisel to make traveling room for the saw.

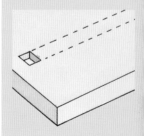

3 Lay out dadoes using the spacing scrap, aligning marks to the scrap fence's end to cut each dado; when done cutting, reglue the edge strip, notching the shelf front to fit around it.

Routed housed rabbet

One shoulder added to a housing joint improves the racking resistance and resolves the problems of fitting a full housing for a clean look. Two shoulders weaken the housed part unnecessarily. For shelving, the housed rabbet is superior to the full housing, but the full housing is a better choice for interior carcass mechanicals like drawer runners. Milled as housed rabbets, they lack the material for milling the screw slots needed to attach them. For a cleaner look when housing these parts, cut a tiny cosmetic shoulder just to cover the joinery line. Drawer frames can use either joint. The method shown allows cutting a full housed rabbet with one straight bit for dadoing and no router fence or any additional rabbeting bit to cut the rabbet.

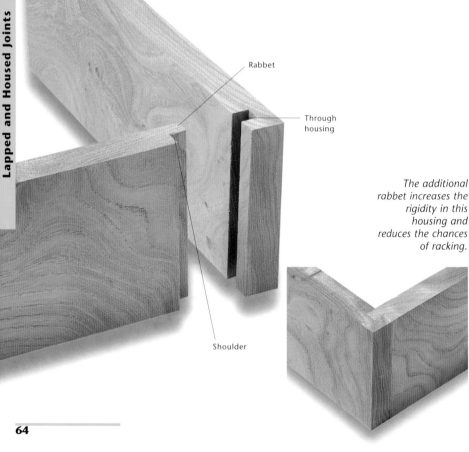

Rabbet

Through housing

Shoulder

The additional rabbet increases the rigidity in this housing and reduces the chances of racking.

Lapped and Housed Joints

Routed Housed Rabbet

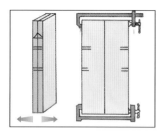

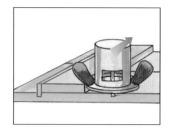

1 Choose a straight bit, two-thirds the shelf thickness. Lay out two dadoes and spacing on mated uprights, then clamp flat and square the marks around.

4 Guide the router against the fence to run the second dado, advancing the fence to each new dado to space successive cuts with the fence clamped in place.

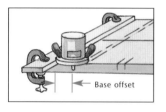

Base offset

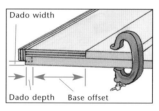

Dado width

Dado depth   Base offset

2 Measure from bit to sub-base edge and offset a fence this distance from the dado layout. Cut the first dado between the marks about a third the thickness.

5 Make another gauge equaling the base offset plus the dado depth and use it to set a fence for rabbeting tongues on the shelf ends that fit the dado's width.

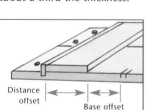

Distance offset

Base offset

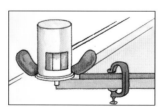

3 Fit a runner snugly into the dado, then measure from it to the next dado, subtract the base offset, rip a fence to this width and attach it to the runner.

6 Cut rabbets on each end so the distance between shelf shoulders equals the desired dimension between uprights and the tongues don't keep shoulders from seating.

Housed Rabbet Variations A

half or single-shouldered dovetail is the easiest housed dovetail to make, but since it slides in from the back, it's sometimes difficult to get the parts in over a long dado when they swell with glue.

Housing a rabbet at a board's end for certain corner joints isn't as strong as a dovetail overall, but placed in tension at a cabinet bottom or drawer corner, the housed rabbet is a serviceable joint if the short grain is sufficient and the drawer bottom or cabinet back reduces racking. Its close cousin, the tongue-and-lap, improves on the problem of a corner-housed rabbet's invisible end grain.

Routed Housed Rabbet

Stop-routed housed rabbet

The beauty of through housings is their faster fabrication; the drawback is the joinery showing. A housed rabbet cut through isn't particularly pretty at the front edge of a structure. A face frame will cover it, but it takes additional time to make. Thus, the choice between a through housing or the "slower" stopped housing becomes a matter of design.

Aligning the cut to the layout and stopping the dado with a saddle jig is convenient. The jig better controls staying on the line and stopping at the right spot; it improves accuracy and reduces the stress of working.

This is the ultimate housing joint, combining strength and clean lines when assembled.

Shoulder

Stopped housing

Stop-Routed Housed Rabbet

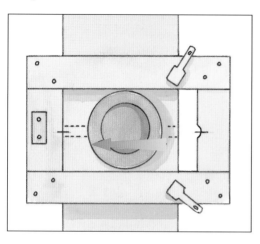

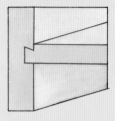

1 Align the saddle jig center line to the dado center line and set a block to stop the router just short of the front edge of the dado stock.

Half Dovetails
When outward forces are expected (like the weight of leaning books on a tall case), a half dovetail tongue reinforces the joint against tension.

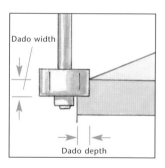

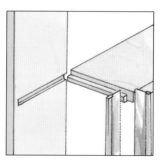

2 Cut the rabbets with a rabbeting bit whose cutting depth equals the dado depth, and rout down until the tongue thickness fits the dado width snugly.

3 Saw away a length of the tongue to match the set-back of the stopped dado, pare the shoulder there, and test that the front edges of the joint align flush.

Drawer Joints
The housed rabbet joins cabinet tops and bottoms to the sides and drawer backs and fronts to their sides if drawer-front end grain will be covered by an attached face.

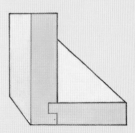

ABOUT THE MORTISE-AND-TENON

There are two basic tenon types that mate with two basic mortise types. A through tenon fits into a through mortise, a hole right through the mortised part. A stub or blind tenon fits into a blind mortise, one which bottoms in the material of the mortised part instead of passing through it. Mortise shapes are mostly rectilinear, round, or a long slot with rounded ends.

An open slot mortise is a relative of the mortise-and-tenon.

The shoulders that are added to the tenon serve several purposes. They increase rack resistance to stabilize the joint. They move the tenon (and with it the mortise) away from the weaker ends or edges of mortised parts. They cover the joint's edges and create a depth stop. Both tenon shoulders and mortises can be angled to modify the basic T or L square orientation of the mortise-and-tenon.

Mortise-and-Tenon Terminology

The pocket of the mortise accepts a projecting tongue or tenon.

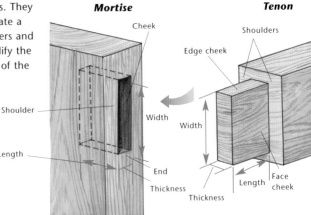

Mortise

Cheek
Shoulder
Length
End
Thickness

Tenon

Shoulders
Edge cheek
Width
Width
Length
Thickness
Face cheek

The Basic Types of Mortise

A blind mortise has a flat bottom that stops short of the opposite face, and the tenon end is therefore enclosed by the wood.

A through mortise makes a hole through the material, and once the joint is assembled, the tenon end can be seen on the other side of the hole.

The specialized slot mortise is nothing more than a deep dado cut in the end of the part, and is used in slip or bridle joints, mortise-and-tenon relatives.

The Basic Types of Tenon

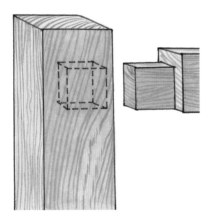

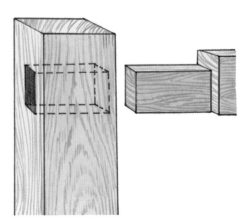

A blind or stub tenon is enclosed by a blind mortise and doesn't pass through the mortised part.

A through tenon inserted in a through mortise extends at least to the opposite face of the mortised part and sometimes beyond it.

The Basic Types of Tenon Shoulders

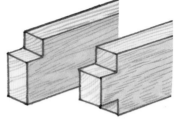

A tenon is barefaced when there are no shoulders on the face sides, which directs its use to slats or thin material that would be weakened by cutting shoulders.

Cutting one or two edge shoulders on a barefaced tenon increases the rack resistance, sets an exact length on the part, and makes a positive depth stop.

A single front shoulder makes a tenon resemble an end lap and offsets it for certain applications, but the tenon is still considered barefaced.

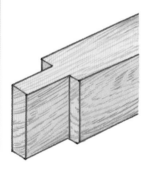

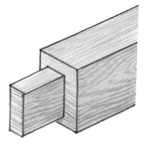

A tenon with two front shoulders is the perfect mate for a slot mortise, but in through or blind mortises it lacks edge shoulders to hide overlong mortise ends.

A third shoulder moves a tenon and its mating mortise away from a frame corner so that both mortise and tenon are enclosed by wood in the joint.

Four shoulders are difficult to align around the entire part and are often unnecessary in construction, except when the joint will be carved or shaped after assembly.

The Evolution of Joint Families

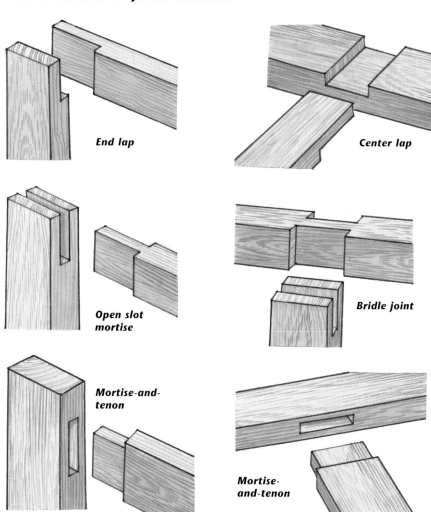

End lap

Center lap

Open slot mortise

Bridle joint

Mortise-and-tenon

Mortise-and-tenon

In the corner L orientation, it's easy to see the evolution of joint families from end laps to slot mortises to mortise-and-tenon joints.

Laps in the T orientation, slot mortised bridle joints, and mortise-and-tenon joints have a doubled glue surface and an increased resistance to racking.

Choosing and using mortise and tenon

There are hundreds of variations of the mortise-and-tenon. In each design, whether a frame, leg assembly, or carcass joint, the requirements change, and the joint is modified to meet them. Variations take into consideration the material, the mortise type, and mating tenon for structure and style. Other factors include the shoulder suited to joint stability and design, and the reinforcements needed against stress.

Tenons are weakest against tension. Without the glue bond, they are easy to pull out of the mortise. Pinning or wedging prevents this and adds mechanical strength to the joint. Pinning is simple: just a dowel, screw, or peg through the assembled joint and maybe a decorative plug at the surface. But over long years of wood movement, pinning risks splitting the mortised part without a film finish to slow down moisture exchange. Wedging, if the mortise is splayed or the tenon is run through and itself mortised for a wedge or key, creates a resistance to tension that is unlikely to fail unless the material is destroyed.

Modifications to tenons and shoulders are the main tactics used to stabilize the joint against twisting and racking. Sometimes a tenon design will stabilize the project itself. Certain tenon designs have evolved and have been refined to fill specific needs, such as the haunch used in frame-and-panel construction, which fills the panel groove showing in the end of the stile. Mortise-and-tenon leg and stretcher joints also have histories, ranging from medieval traveling trestle tables, run through and "tusked" or wedged without glue for easy disassembly, to bridle joints used to join the front legs and apron of classic demi-lune tables.

Reinforcing Mortise-and-Tenon Against Tension

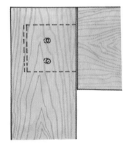

Pins inserted through an assembled bridle joint reinforce against loading and tension, while pins into a draw-bored mortise-and-tenon pull the joint tight by aligning slightly offset holes.

Stabilizing the Mortise-and-Tenon

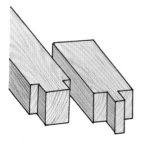

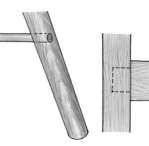

A thick tenon may resist twist but remove too much mortise material; a thin one is weaker and has too much end grain that won't be supported by gluing.

In a frame, the panel groove is filled by a haunch, giving rack resistance like a shoulder plus twist resistance while keeping the tenon back from the end.

When a tenoned stretcher lacking shoulder area is run through and wedged, it gains rack resistance built into a wide-shouldered tenon with a large long-grain glue area.

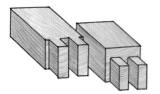

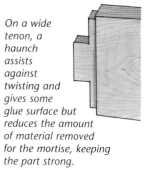

Twin tenons, whose mortises should run lengthwise with the grain, greatly improve against twist, and work even better against rack with an edge shoulder.

Tongued shoulders assist the stability of the joint and the material by restraining movement near the surface.

On a wide tenon, a haunch assists against twisting and gives some glue surface but reduces the amount of material removed for the mortise, keeping the part strong.

Choosing and Using Mortise and Tenon

Tenon wedge patterns

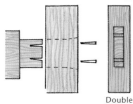

Double | Single center | Edge | Diagonal

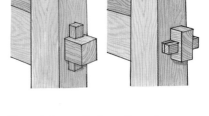

To tighten or splay the tenon so it can't be withdrawn, through tenons are slotted to received wedges, and the mortise is sometimes tapered wider on the side opposite insertion.

Through tenons that are themselves mortised to receive single- or double-tapered wedges reinforce against tension. The wedges are removable for disassembly.

The Mortise-and-Tenon in Carcasses

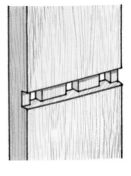

Drawer rails are commonly stub-tenoned into the side of the carcass when the structure doesn't require them to hold the sides in against bowing.

In a variation of a housed joint, a full or partial housing is mortised and mating tenons are cut in the shelf end or tongue.

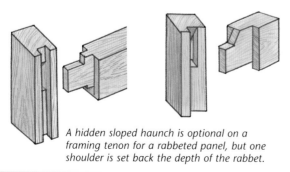

Tenons without face shoulder can be run through and wedged to join shelves to carcass sides.

The Mortise-and-Tenon in Frames

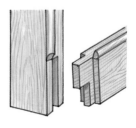

A hidden sloped haunch is optional on a framing tenon for a rabbeted panel, but one shoulder is set back the depth of the rabbet.

A moulded edge frame can be rabbeted or grooved to receive the panel, but the moulding is mitered to continue around the inside.

The Mortise-and-Tenon in Leg Assemblies

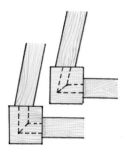

 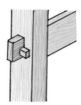

Stretcher tenons can extend beyond the mortise for decoration or for function, as in a trestle table's wedged through tenon.

To join chair seat rails to angle in toward the back, the tenon is angled if it can retain some continuous long grain, or the mortise is angled instead.

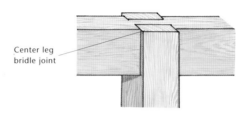

Center leg bridle joint

The bridle joint is commonly used to allow the apron to run through a center table leg, or to join the foot of a trestle table.

 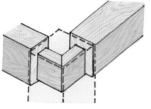

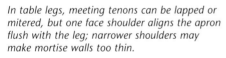

Trestle table foot

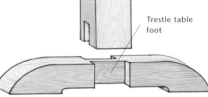

In table legs, meeting tenons can be lapped or mitered, but one face shoulder aligns the apron flush with the leg; narrower shoulders may make mortise walls too thin.

A separate loose, or slip, tenon simplifies shoulder cuts and fitting; mortises are machined with one bit and tenons cut from a strip of material.

The short-grain weakness of arched rails where they meet the stiles is solved by angling tenon shoulders, or the tenon itself is modified to meet the requirements of the joint.

Basic mortise-and-tenon

The standard width of a mortise in edge grain is about one-third the stock thickness. This proportion varies since the mortise is usually matched to the mortising chisel closest to one-third the stock thickness. Too wide a mortise and the cheeks are weak; too narrow and the tenon is weak, so this proportion is a general guide. Chopping a mortise entirely by hand takes practice for accurate results. Scribing the layout lines deeper once they are placed lets the first chisel cuts remove the waste cleanly, leaving a good guide shoulder for the chisel. Chiseling tiny bevels in the mortise waste also helps to guide a good chop.

One school of thought on sawing tenons holds that first sawing the shoulders could weaken the tenon by severing long-grain if the sawing goes too deep. On the other hand, sawing the cheeks first is preferred when a part is tenoned at both ends because the shoulders establish the length.

Cut all mortises and then fit tenons to them. It's much easier to shave a little off a tenon cheek than a mortise cheek.

Tenon

Mortise

Shoulder

Making a Blind Mortise by Hand

1 With trued faces and edges aligned, outline the tenon part onto the mortise part, leaving a temporary horn to prevent splitting if the mortise falls at a corner.

4 Referencing from the marked face, adjust the gauge fence to position the mortise width on the stock thickness. Scribe it between the squared end lines.

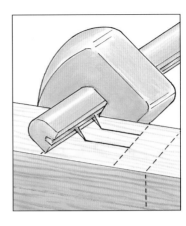

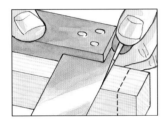

2 Locate the mortise length within the outline of the tenon part, insetting for any shoulders. Scribe each mortise end square across from the trued face with a knife.

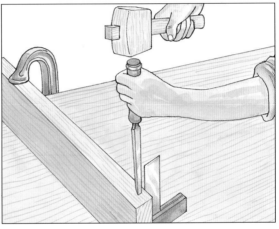

5 Clamp the part over a bench leg and stand a square nearby to visually aid holding the sides and back of the mortise chisel at 90° to the work.

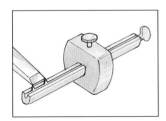

3 Set the spurs of the mortise marking gauge to the chisel width nearest one third the stock thickness; leave at least a quarter of the stock for each mortise cheek.

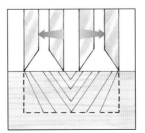

6 One chopping method starts the cuts at the center, and they increase in depth as the chisel moves toward the mortise ends and is reversed for the paring end cut.

VARIATIONS

Other Methods for Blind Mortising

The alternative to clearing the waste with a mortising chisel is to drill it out and clean up the cheeks with bench chisels. A brad-point bit or Forstner bit works fine, but the Forstner leaves a flat bottom that makes it simple to gauge the depth of the mortise.

Routers can be set up to mortise horizontally, but some simpler solutions are shown opposite. Bits must have a capacity for end cutting, and up-spiral flutes help to clear the chips from the mortise. Several shallow passes are best.

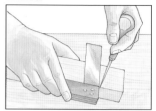

7 In a second method, the chisel chops part way down and leverages the waste on along the mortise and down another layer until last cuts pare waste at the ends.

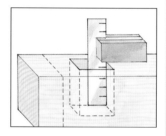

8 Clean up the bottom by leveraging with the chisel and extend a square to check that cheeks are flat and square to the face and that the depth is correct.

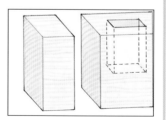

9 Trim the ends to their mark with a last paring cut to clean up any marred edges from leveraging. Glue the joint, then saw off the horn.

Basic Tenon by Hand

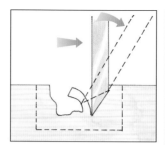

1 From the trued edge, scribe a shoulder square across the face, then square the line around, marking all shoulders and tenon length to fit the mortise depth.

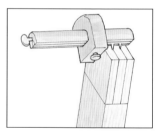

2 Set the mortise marking gauge slightly over the mortise width and adjust the fence to locate and score the tenon thickness around the part from the marked face.

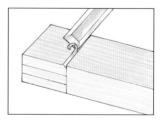

3 Score the shoulder lines deeper and use a chisel to pare a small bevel along the waste of the face shoulders to guide the saw.

Mortise-and-Tenon

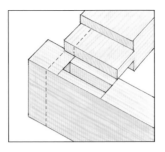

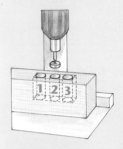

4 Hold the part and the cleat of a bench hook between thumb and fingers and use the index finger to steady the saw, then saw the shoulder to the tenon line.

7 Align the tenon to the mortise layout and mark the cutting line for the third shoulder, gauging each successive part from its own mortise.

Forstner Bits Use a Forstner bit to clear the waste and reference a flat bottom, plunging the mortise at each end and then the middle, clearing further with the bit and chisels.

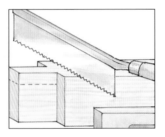

5 Clamp the tenon upright and tilted away to saw down the layout lines, steadying the saw with a thumb to keep the kerf in the waste side of the material.

8 Cut the third shoulder down to the marked line, being careful not to saw into the face shoulders, then saw along the tenon grain and remove the waste.

Routing Mortises Guide a plunge router along the mortise part while it is clamped in the bench vise and raised flush with another board for clearance and extra router support.

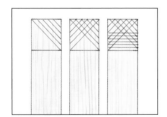

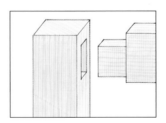

6 The first cuts make a kerf that guides the second cut when the part is reversed in the vise for sawing; a third cut removes the remainder.

9 Pare the tenon with bench chisels to fit the mortise with hand pressure, or use a rabbet plane to smooth saw marks and seat the shoulders.

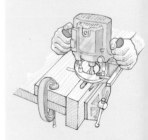

Basic Mortise and Tenon

Open slot mortise on a radial-arm saw

Making an open slot mortise on the radial-arm saw has the advantage of working the part horizontally when it might be too long or heavy for vertical cutting on the table saw with a tenoning jig like those shown in this chapter. The mortise width follows the one-third general rule, but it is gauged and marked on the end and down each edge to the tenon width, marked like a shoulder.

Sometimes known as a bridle joint, the open slot mortise-and-tenon can be likened to a center lap with three equal divisions.

Shoulder

Cheek

Open slot Mortise

Open Slot Mortise on a Radial-Arm Saw

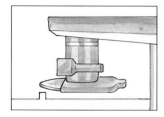

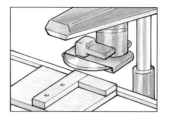

1 Lock a dado head of the desired mortise width in the horizontal position so the outer diameter of the blade aligns exactly with the front of the saw fence.

2 Make a sliding jig from scrap plywood and attach a fence square across it plus a scrap to prevent hand slippage into the blade.

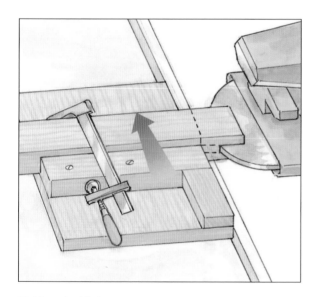

3 Align the blade to waste the mortise by sliding the jig past the blade while feeding the part into it until the marked shoulder lines up with the saw fence's edge.

Alternative Methods

Handsaw an open slot mortise on the center waste side of the layout. An alternative to drilling a hole to release the waste is to chop it out with a chisel after sawing. Working from each side toward the center, chop down into the waste and split pieces out from the end grain. A cleaner way to do this is to use a Forstner bit in a drill press, with a fence adjusted so that the drill is exactly aligned on the center of the mortise. With care, the holes can break into each other, leaving very little material to finally be pared out with a bench chisel. Support the work on a piece of scrap to prevent tear-out.

Open Slot Mortise on a Radial-Arm Saw

Through mortise by hand

The only cautions for through mortising by hand (besides staying square to the face) is against tear-out on the side not covered by tenon shoulders. For this reason, the layout is carried around and worked from each side toward the center.

To help prevent tear-out when cutting through mortises, first scribe the through mortise layout deep into the shouldered side. This might allow drilling straight through from the opposite side without tear-out. If the part is drilled from both sides, use a fence to position the layout under the bit and keep the same face against the fence for precise alignment.

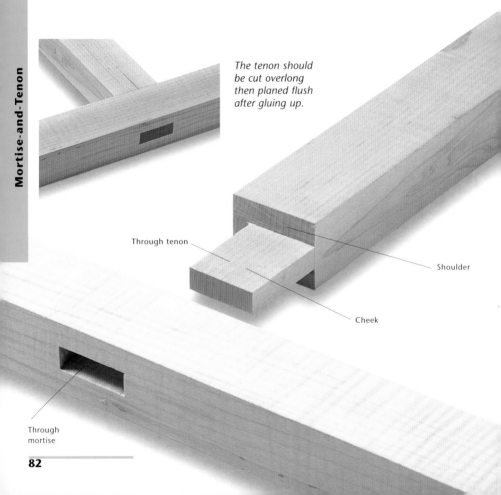

The tenon should be cut overlong then planed flush after gluing up.

Through tenon

Shoulder

Cheek

Through mortise

Through Mortise by Hand

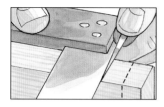

1 Follow the mortise layout steps on page 77, but this time square the scribed mortise end lines around the part to the opposite face.

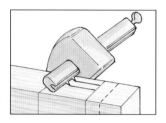

2 Again following those layout steps, mark the mortise width with a gauge, but also mark the width on the opposite face, referencing the fence against the same face while marking.

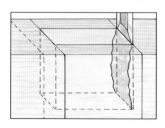

3 Work from each face toward the middle. Chop the waste and form a slight crown of waste at each end to pare slightly and square to the face to finish.

More Mortising Techniques

Routing Angled Mortises To use a router jig for angled mortises, mark the mortise angle on the part and adjust the jig until the mortise is square to the table, then rout it out.

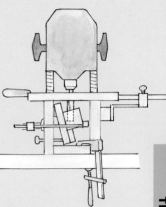

Clearing Through Mortises Clear through mortise waste by drilling part way through from each side with a brad-point bit, then pare the cheeks flat using a chisel.

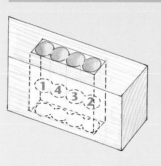

Clearing Slot Mortise Waste Drill a hole at the bottom of the slot mortise so the waste will release when the slot is sawn following procedures for tenon sawing on page 79.

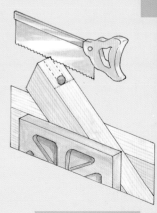

Angled mortise and tenon

When an angled mortise is transferred from a full-size drawing to the part, the mortise width and ends are still scribed into the working edge. The same angled fixture shown for the drill press works for chopping by hand with the chisel kept vertical.

An overhand routing box can be used to cut angled mortises. Similar to a hand miter box without saw slots, such a fixture can be modified with a hinged ledge set by a thumbscrew for holding the part to be mortised. Set the angle from a drawing and mark it on the end, adjusting the part until the mortise sides are square to the bench top. Mortises angled longitudinally must be tilted up square, as when drilling out waste on the drill press. To rout a mortise with such a fixture the part is clamped to one side of the box while the router rides on top and its fence bears on one side.

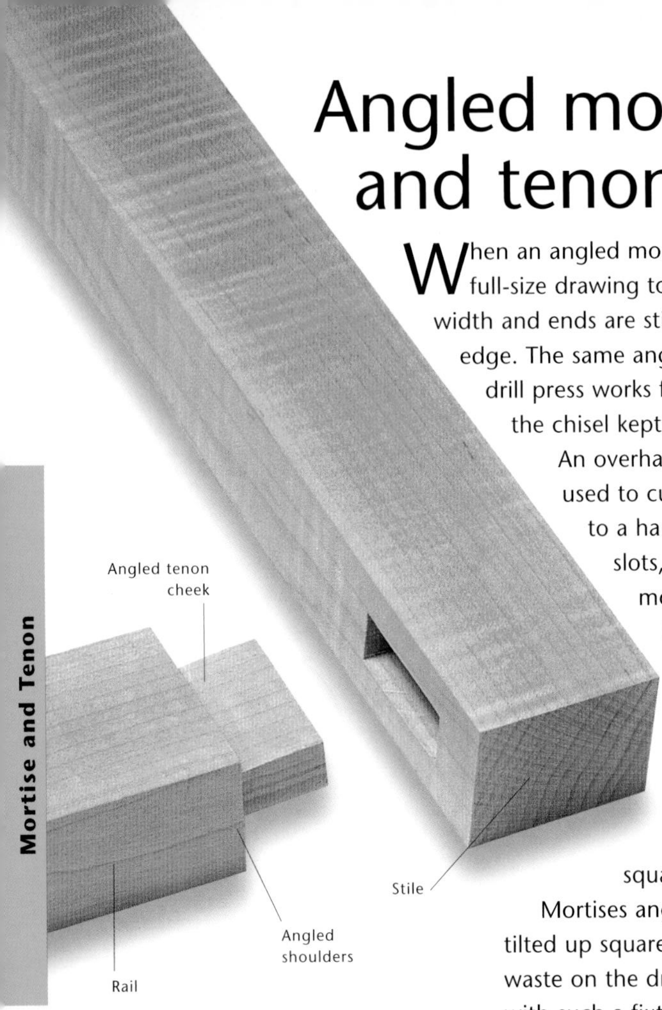

Angled tenon cheek

Stile

Angled shoulders

Rail

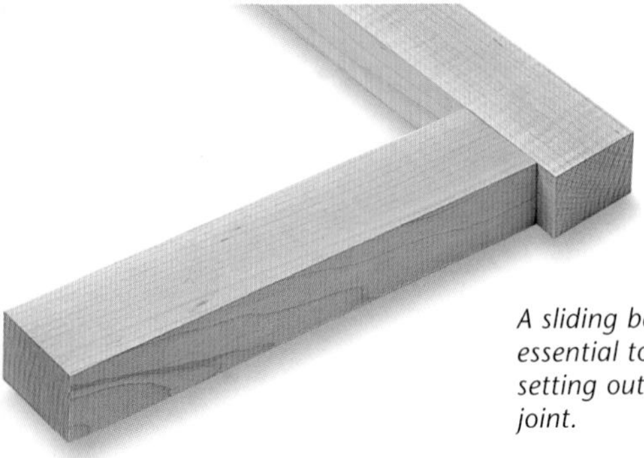

A sliding bevel is an essential tool for setting out this joint.

Angled Mortise on a Drill Press

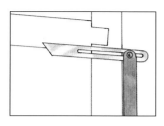

1 From a full-sized drawing of the joint, set a bevel square to the angle of the mortise and use it to mark the angle on the outside of the real part.

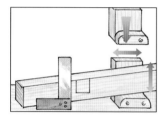

2 Slide a stepped block with a rounded shoulder to prevent marring along the length of the part, elevating it until the mortise layout is square to the bench top.

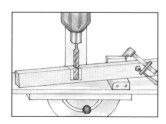

3 Clamp the block in place, supporting the assembly on an auxiliary table if necessary; set the bit depth from the marked layout and waste the mortise, then pare it clean.

Other Tenoning Methods The methods for machining basic tenons are similar to those for making end laps. The only difference is in the layout and cutter adjustment since two cheeks are usually cut instead of one. The adjustable jig that rides in the miter gauge slot is a variation of the fenced straddling jig shown earlier. Runners in grooves between the halves of the jig keep it square.

Stop Blocks A stop block on the table saw fence sets the cut for the shoulder, and the cheek is wasted by running it over a dado head raised to the shoulder width.

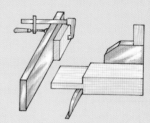

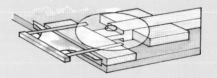

Wasting Tenon Cheeks A router can waste tenon cheeks using a jig made of scrap wood attached to plywood to hold the part and support the router, which is stopped at the shoulder by its edge guide.

Tenoning Jigs After first kerfing shoulders with a table saw blade lowered to shoulder width, an adjustable tenoning jig can ride in the miter gauge slot to waste each cheek from the outside.

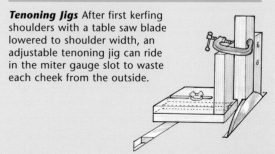

Angled Tenon

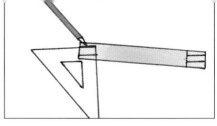

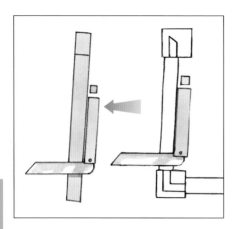

1 Transfer the edge shoulder angle with a sliding bevel from the full-sized drawing to overlong stock, marking the shoulders the correct distance apart.

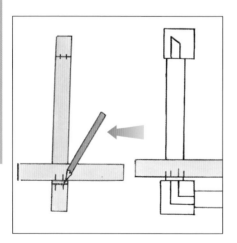

2 Measure or use a story stick to transfer the mortise offset and tenon thickness from the drawing to the part on the angled shoulder marks.

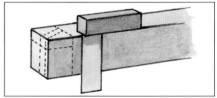

3 Align the square corner of an architect's triangle to the shoulder mark and extend the marks for the tenon thickness along the part's edge.

4 Square the face shoulders across and connect the edge shoulder angle on the opposite edge. Extend tenon outline from that angle, mark tenon thickness, and saw.

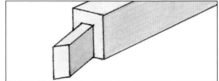

5 For mitered tenons, after the tenon and third shoulder are cut, mark the tenon length and use an architect's triangle to scribe the miter cut on the tenon end at 45° to the shoulder.

6 Trim off the tenon end and clean up the cheeks and shoulders as done for any other tenon.

Mortise-and-Tenon

Through wedged tenon

When the load on a structure puts the mortise-and-tenon in tension, the glue bond is the only thing that keeps the joint together unless the joint is reinforced. Pinning, wedging, and wedging with a key or tusk are the basic methods for increasing resistance to tension on the joint.

Splaying the existing side of a through mortise and kerfing the tenon for one or more wedges are a sure sign of durable hand joinery. Run wedges of a contrasting wood across the grain of the mortise to keep it from splitting. Make each wedge no wider than the tenon thickness. For thicker wedges, remove small sections of the tenon in a shallow V shape.

Saw cuts

Drilled holes

Provides strength with great resistance to failure as the wedges force the tenon to form a dovetail.

Wedges

Through Wedged Tenon

More about Reinforcements

To cut wedges on a table saw, use a simple piece of plywood scrap with the wedge taper cut into the edge like a notch. With the workpiece in the notch, the plywood can run along the fence as the blade cuts the wedge. Such a jig can also position work for a handsaw. Wedges are always cut with the grain. Otherwise tapping in will snap them. The architect's triangle simplifies layout and doubles as a tool for setting the angle of saw blades.

Pins through the joint should be placed near the shoulder because they restrict wood movement and eventually may split in the mortise part if the species isn't very stable. Keep the diameter of the reinforcing pins small, but larger flush round plugs or round or square pegheads left sticking out can be used for a decorative accent.

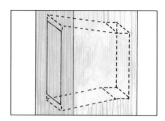

1 Add about ⅟₁₆" (0.16 cm) to each end of the mortise length and taper the end cheeks toward the front, leaving a flat where the tenon enters.

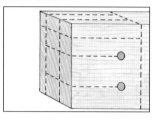

2 Lay out tenon cheeks, shoulders, and wedge locations, then drill a small hole about a quarter of the tenon length from the shoulder to locate the bottom of each wedge slot.

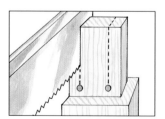

3 First saw the tenon cheeks and shoulders, then saw down the cheek to the small holes that will prevent splitting when the wedges are inserted.

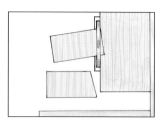

4 Make the jig described in the sidebar to cut wedges with the grain from stock the same thickness as the tenon, flipping stock for each cut.

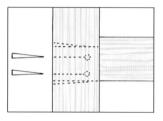

5 Glue the joint and clamp the shoulders home temporarily until the cheeks are clamped, then tap the glued wedges in, alternating taps so they penetrate to equal depths.

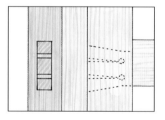

6 When the glue is dry, remove the clamp from the cheeks and saw off any projecting wedges, then sand or plane the joint flush.

Draw-bored tenon

Tenons can be draw-bored for a tapered pin so tapping home draws the joint tight. Sometimes the taper is square and pounded in to lock in the material. If draw-boring is used on a slot mortise, align the second hole to pull the tenon in and down in the mortise. Draw-boring is more likely to appear in the likes of rustic furniture, green wood projects, or timber framing than in refined work.

Pin

Offset hole

The pin will pull the tenon tightly home if drilled correctly.

Draw-Bored Tenon

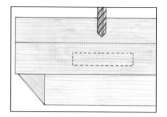

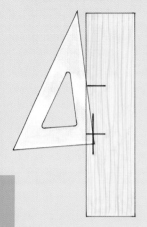

Cutting Wedges To make a wedge-cutting jig, mark the length and thickness of the wedge slot, extending beyond the points with an architect's triangle, then cut out its corner outlines.

1 Lay out the mortise and back it up with scrap to drill a hole at the center of the mortise length, back about a quarter the stock width from the edge.

Pinning Joints After the joint is glued and dried, pin it by drilling through the mortise part close to the tenon shoulder. Insert dowel with glue and trim it flush.

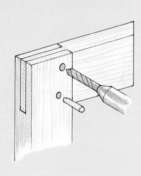

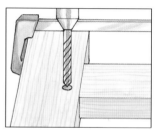

2 After cutting the mortise-and-tenon as usual, assemble and clamp the joint, then insert the drill bit into the hole just to mark its locations on the tenon.

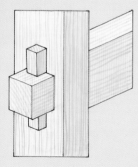

Tusked Tenons A tusked tenon can be assembled with glue, or without it if the furniture is designed for disassembly.

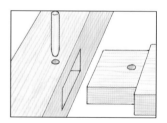

3 Drill a hole in the tenon slightly closer to the shoulder than to the bit mark, then assemble the joint and drive a tapered peg into it.

Angled tenon and shoulder

Angled tenons or shoulders are common where stretchers join tapered or canted table legs and where chair seat rails and stretchers join chair legs. Full-sized drawings are indispensable aids for setting up layout tools and determining measurements when joinery angles vary from 90°.

The edge or face shoulders of an angled tenon aren't square to the stock, but the tenon is usually laid out square to the angled shoulder so the mortise can be made square to its stock. Its angled shoulder turns the tenon oblique to the grain. An angled tenon must contain some continuous long grain for strength. Drawings help to visualize this and work out the size of tenon within the stock dimensions.

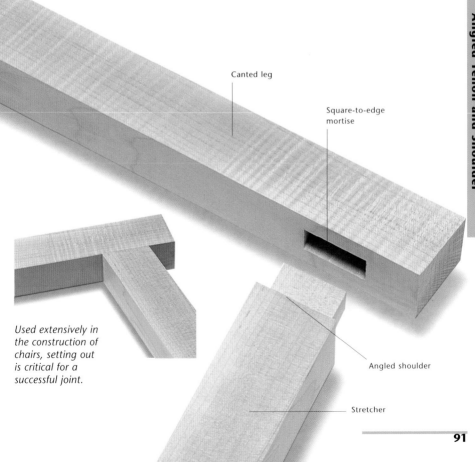

Canted leg

Square-to-edge mortise

Used extensively in the construction of chairs, setting out is critical for a successful joint.

Angled shoulder

Stretcher

Angled Shoulder

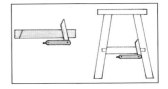

More Angled Tenons Handsaw or bandsaw angled tenons like any other. On the radial-arm saw, turn the blade horizontal and use a height table under the part. The tilt direction of table saws vary, and so might the height of tenon shoulders from the table. Either tilt the blade and use a vertical tenoning jig, or keep the blade vertical and tilt the part.

To cut angled tenons with a router, use an angled router step jig with two tiers and cleats underneath to align the part for wasting the tenon cheeks to the shoulder. The second tier is set back the distance from the outer diameter of the bit to the edge of the router sub-base. Do this by careful measuring or more simply by attaching the second tier slightly farther back and then have it guide the router to trim the edge of the first tier exactly in line with the bit.

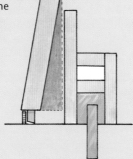

Using Wedges Taking the taper angle from full-size plans, set the tenon cheek angle with a wood wedge on a vertical fence sliding jig.

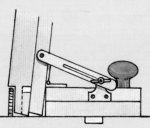

Hinged Jigs After kerfing the shoulders, align the tenon cheek layout to the blade with an adjustable tilting hinged jig that runs in the miter gauge slot.

Stepped Jigs To cut cheeks with a router use a stepped jig cut to the shoulder angle; the router is guided and stopped by the step on the jig.

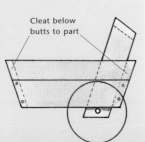

Cleat below
butts to part

1 Cut the stock to length and transfer the shoulder angle and location from the full-sized drawing to it, then use the angle to set the miter gauge on the table saw.

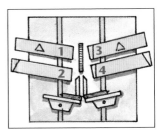

2 Raise a dado head to shoulder width and waste cheek 1, flip the stock for cheek 2, then reset the miter gauge on the right to cut cheeks 3 and 4.

3 Saw down the tenon to trim it to width and across the edge shoulders, following the angle, to release the waste.

Mortise and Tenon

Slip, or loose, tenon

It's easy to confuse the name "slip tenon" with an open slot mortise or slip joint and the name "loose tenon" with a through tenon that is reinforced with a key or tusk but not glued. The same terms refer to different joints. Here a slip or loose tenon is a joint composed of two mortised parts bridged by a separate, floating tenon.

Loose tenons are based on machine joinery techniques. A round bit whose diameter equals the mortise width is plunged in at one end of the mortise, moved along the mortise length to cut it, and pulled out, leaving a rounded mortise end. Confusingly, this type of mortise is called a slot mortise, but is not the same as the open slot mortise.

Slip tenon

Slot mortise

Slip tenon

Slot mortise

An efficient method for repairing broken tenons in furniture restoration.

Round Tenons and Round Stock Round tenons are also made loose by drilling into both parts and using dowel pins or doweling rod as tenons. To make an integral round tenon, center a plug cutter on the part's end on the drill press or lathe after kerfing in the shoulders.

One method is shown opposite for routing a round-end tenon horizontally, but vertical routing is possible with ball-bearing rabbeting bits and a jig. The work is done either end up with the part held stationary and the router handheld and moving, or end down with the part held by a move-able jig and the bit stationary in a router table. Drilling for a round tenon is fairly straightforward, but by using a V-block for marking and holding, a round part can be mortised convent-ionally and a flat shoulder chiseled to accept a rectangular shoulder.

Slip, or Loose, Tenon

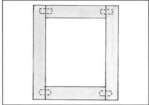

1 Make a full-size drawing to determine the part widths and lengths and mortise-and-tenon placement, then cut the stiles to length and the rails to the length between them.

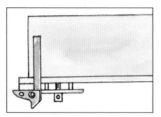

2 Clamp one corner's rail vertically in the vise and line up its stile horizontally to mark mortises simultaneously on the rail end and stile edge, and repeat for each corner.

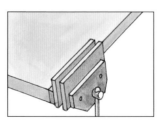

3 Set up for one of the methods shown on pages 77–78, in this case auxiliary vise jaws attached through the bolt holes and extending the jaw height.

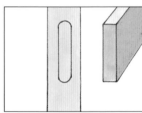

4 Clamp the workpiece flush with the vise jaws, align an end-cutting straight bit with the router edge guide set against the jaw, and cut each mortise in several passes.

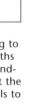

5 Mill a length of tenon stock that is as wide as the length of the mortise and as thick as the width of it.

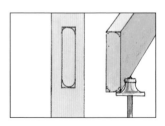

6 Match the tenon stock to the mortise either by squaring the mortise corners or by rounding the edges of the tenon stock.

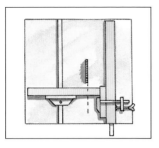

7 Set up a stop block on the saw fence to repeat cut tenons that are slightly less than double the depth of the mortise.

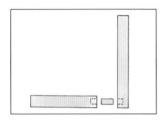

8 Spread glue in the mortises and on the tenon and assemble each joint, then clamp the frame.

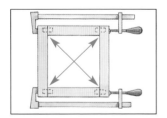

9 Adjust the clamps until each diagonal measures the same, ensuring that the frame is square. Let the frame dry undisturbed.

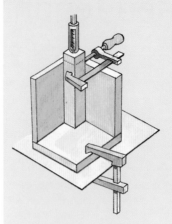

Corner Jigs Using a corner jig that lowers with the drill press table is one way to end-cut with a plug cutter to make a round tenon after shoulders have been kerfed.

V-Block Holes
An oversize hole in a V-block lets a router table straight bit through to cut the tenon and also allows adjustment from the fence stop to control tenon length.

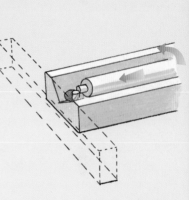

Round Mortises
Clamp round stock in a V-block to drill round mortises, or slide a marking device along the edge to make parallel lines for a conventional style of mortise.

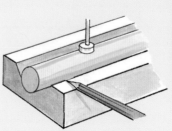

Slip, or Loose, Tenon

Haunched tenon

Edge and face shoulders on a tenon increase its mechanical resistance to racking. But each shoulder reduces the material in the tenon and replaces it with the shoulder's end grain, which lacks gluing strength. Deep edge shoulders subtract gluing area from the tenon's cheek and make a wide part vulnerable to twisting, which easily breaks the shoulder's end-grain bond. Wood movement and shrinking in the joint also stress the glue bond. Haunches and multiple tenons help to overcome these difficulties.

Mortise-and-Tenon

The haunch provides a greater glue area when used at the end of stock.

Haunch

Haunched Tenon

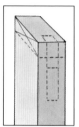

1 Gauge the mortise width on the edge and horn end, making a depth there equal to the mortise width, and start the mortise its own width away from the horn cut-off line.

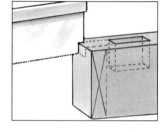

2 Chop the mortise, saw along the lines extending from it on the horn edge and down the horn end to the depth marked.

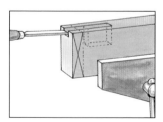

3 Tap a chisel lightly into the end grain between the sawn lines to chip out the waste down to the depth mark, paring the bottom parallel to the face.

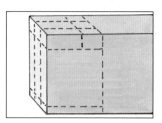

4 Lay out the tenon to fit the mortise and scribe the haunch line across the outside edge forward of the face shoulders an amount equal to the tenon's thickness.

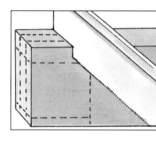

5 Saw down the haunch line to the tenon, then saw the face and bottom edge shoulders, and the cheeks.

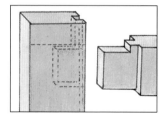

6 Test fit the tenon, making sure neither the haunch nor the tenon length prevent the shoulders from seating, then glue the joint and cut off the horn.

More Stabilizing Tenons

Haunching and dividing wide tenons is another way to preserve the resistance of the tenon against twisting without mortising out a lot of material. Mortises for the tenons are overlaid by a second shallow mortise for the haunch. The tenon is made normally after the haunch has been marked and cut to fit the shallow mortise. It may be easiest to divide the tenon by cope sawing to the same depth as the haunch.

Twin tenons usually appear on stock more square than rectangular in cross-section. They keep the tenon base wide against twisting, double the glue surface, and proportion the tenons and shoulders to the stock. Orient twin tenons so that the load is on the tenon edge, not the face.

Haunched Tenon

Sloped haunched tenon

More important than fitting the panel groove through the stile's end in frame-and-panel construction, the second shallow mortise that houses the haunch lets the edge shoulder into the wood without weakening the end of the part when the tenon falls there. This creates cheeks for long-grain gluing, one of the main purposes of any woodworking joint. The edge shoulders and tenon are then supported mechanically against twisting and are properly bonded to the mortise cheeks.

Mortise and Tenon

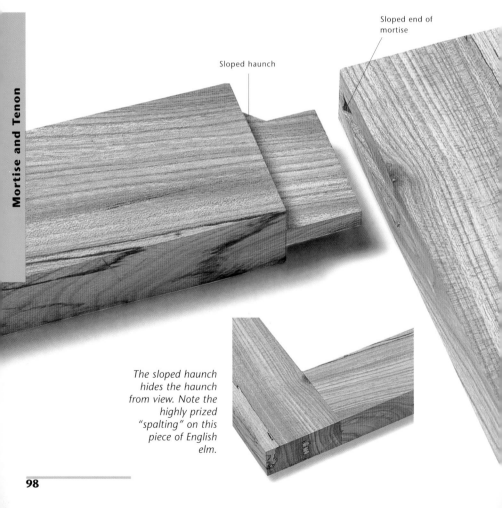

Sloped end of mortise

Sloped haunch

The sloped haunch hides the haunch from view. Note the highly prized "spalting" on this piece of English elm.

Sloped Haunched Tenon

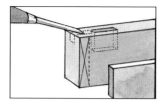

1 Lay out and chop the mortise as for a haunched tenon, then chisel from inside the horn cut-off line, angling down toward the mortise, to reach a depth equal to the mortise width.

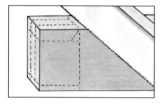

2 Lay out the tenon and make the first saw cut across the top edge angling from the face shoulder line to a measurement from it equal to the tenon thickness.

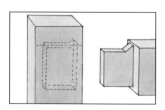

3 Pare the slope slightly down from the top edge (matching its socket started inside the layout), removing material to flush up the parts and conceal the slope.

Reducing Tenon Width
Cut a haunch in a wide tenon and reduce the tenon width to keep the mortise part strong and prevent excessive dimensional conflict from breaking the glue bond.

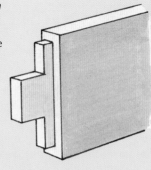

Twin Tenons Set up a router table and push block that runs along the fence to waste each shoulder and between the tenons, thus doubling the gluing surface and increasing the resistance to twisting.

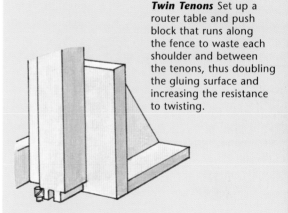

Cutting Kerfs For a tenon that restrains movement of the joint line, cut four saw kerfs for tenon cheeks and shoulders. Then, thin tongues that are shortened, fit to matching slots and glued.

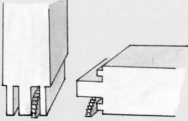

Mortise-and-tenon with panel groove

The basic joint between a frame and panel is a groove housing or a rabbet housing with a stop holding in the panel. The important thing to know is how frame mortise-and-tenons accommodate them.

A groove runs centered on the inside edges of the frame, right over the mortises. The groove width is about one-third the stock thickness, with its depth about the same as its width to keep the material strong. The square profile of a haunch neatly fills the panel groove that runs through the stile's end in frame-and-panel construction.

Mortise-and-Tenon

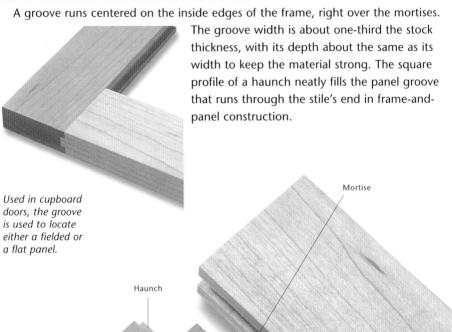

Used in cupboard doors, the groove is used to locate either a fielded or a flat panel.

Mortise

Haunch

Groove to take door panel

Mortise-and-Tenon with Panel Groove

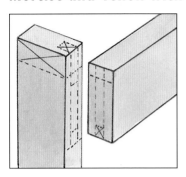

1 Choose a panel groove width, lay out the mortise-and-tenon cheeks to it, mark its depth under the tenon to find the tenon width, and place the mortise.

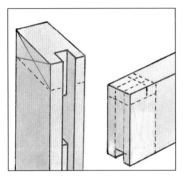

2 Chop the mortise and run the panel groove over it on the inside edges of all parts, then lay out the tenon so the haunch length fills the groove.

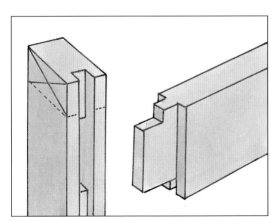

3 Saw the haunch shoulder first, then the face shoulders and tenon cheeks, glue the joint, and saw off the horn.

VARIATIONS

More Framing Tenons Frames for divided panels have tenoned center rails or muntins whose moulded detail will run on both edges. Whether the frame is grooved or rabbeted, to return a moulding around each separate panel the width of the moulding is cut away at the mortise and mitered to match the tenon. Increase the length between tenon shoulders by the width of mouldings cut away. Also increase the length by the amount that mitered tenon shoulders are let into mortise parts to prevent weak short grain on arched rails.

Mortise-and-tenon for a rabbeted frame

The mortise width and tenon thickness match the groove width. Decide this width first and lay out the mortise and tenon cheeks to it. Then mark the groove depth on the end of the tenon stock, allotting the remainder to the tenon and haunch. This determines the length and placement of the mortise on its stock. Mark the frame rabbet on the end of the tenon stock to find the tenon width and so the mortise length and placement. The rabbet should remove about two-thirds of the material thickness to house the panel and stop, and cut into the width of the stock about one-third the thickness or more. The tenon shoulder on the face side of the frame is set back to house the lip formed by rabbeting.

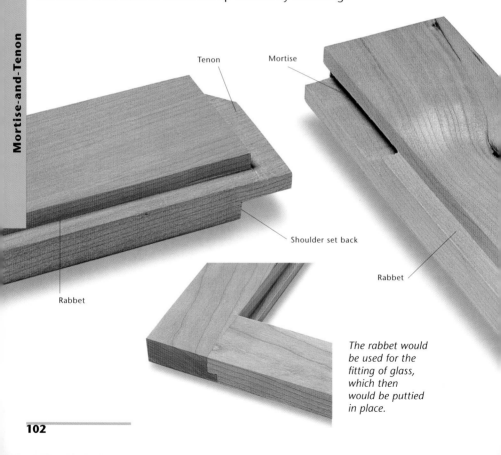

Tenon

Mortise

Shoulder set back

Rabbet

Rabbet

The rabbet would be used for the fitting of glass, which then would be puttied in place.

Mortise-and-Tenon for a Rabbeted Frame

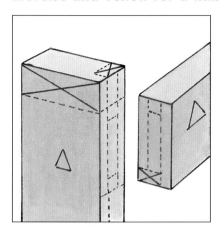

1 Determine the dimensions of the rabbet that will be under the sloped haunch tenon to find the mortise size and placement, then lay out and chop the mortise.

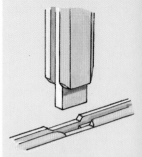

Moulded Details A moulded detail on a frame for several panels is run on both edges of the center rail or muntin like the groove, and the detail is returned by mitering.

2 Run the rabbet to the face side cheeks of the mortise-and-tenon and mark the tenon shoulders, setting the face shoulder back to house the lip left by rabbeting.

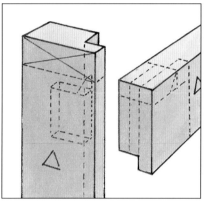

Cutting Miters To prevent weak short grain on an arched rail, a small miter is cut on the shoulder of the tenon and housed in the shoulder of the mortise.

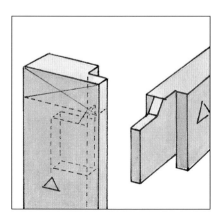

3 Saw the slope of the haunch first, then the two shoulders, the cheeks, and the cuts along the tenon thickness, sawing the horn after the glue dries.

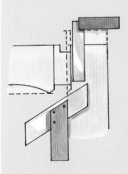

Mortise-and-tenon for a moulded frame

Some frames have a moulded detail on the inside edge that is continued around, or returned, by mitering. After mortising, run a rabbet to a depth equal to the moulding width. But instead of cutting the tenon's face shoulder back to house the lip left on the mortise part, remove the moulded detail flush with the mortise and rabbet, then miter to match the tenon.

Face mould

Miter

Haunch

Make a chisel guide to ensure an accurate mating of the two parts of the mitered moulding.

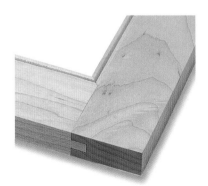

Mortise-and-Tenon for a Moulded Frame

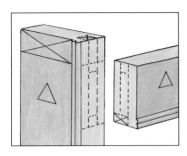

1 Run the moulding detail on the inside face edge of the stock, then lay out the rabbet and haunched tenon mortise so they stop in line with the moulding detail.

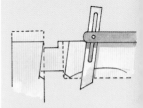

Angled Tenons
Another method for avoiding weak short grain houses a small miter and an angled tenon shoulder within the profile of the mortise part. A particularly elegant way of forming the corner joints of, say, a dining table is the ultimate variation—a mitered mortise and tenon. The 45° miter is cut at both ends of the stiles. The shoulders of the tenons on the rails are cut at 45° also. Edge shoulders are then cut, the tenon length not extending as far as the tips of the miters. The mortise is then carefully worked to suit.

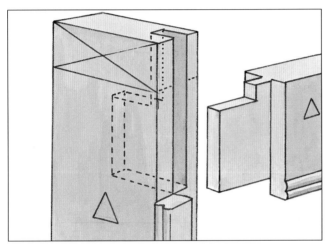

2 Chop the mortise, run the rabbet to the line of the moulding detail, finish the tenon layout and saw it, then saw the moulding detail away flush with the mortise.

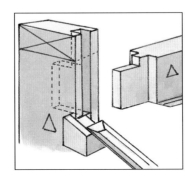

3 Use a 45° chisel guide on the edge of the stock to miter the moulding detail away from the tenon shoulder and mortise, and then fit the joint together.

ABOUT MITERS AND BEVELS

There are three basic types of miters, and they create a fourth type when used in combination. Frame miters angle the blade path across the wood width, but the blade is perpendicular to the face. Cross and length miters angle the blade tilt to the face and are really just bevel cuts. The cross miter path is perpendicular to the wood edge, and the length miter path parallel to it. The fourth type is a compound miter. It combines a bevel tilt with an angled path either across or along the grain.

A mitered corner continues the wood grain visually to harmonize with the design.

The glue surface of a length miter is all long grain, but other miters are weak because the glue surface is end-grain. Consequently, miters need to be reinforced. And even though the gluing orientation is strong, clamp pressure causes miters to slip out of gluing position unless splines or other mechanical restraints are combined with special clamping techniques.

Inaccurate miter joints are hard to get away with and to correct. Time is well spent on adjusting machines and making tests in scraps before committing to the actual cut.

The angle gauges on stationary machines are often imprecise, so miter joints have spawned an aftermarket in precision gauges and jigs, plus an endless array of shop made devices and set-up methods that aid accurate work.

Cutting miters and bevels by machine generates extra force that pulls or pushes the wood, encouraging it to slip out of position during cutting. Sharp blades, hold-downs, stops on the miter gauge, and sandpaper on the face of the wood all reduce the chances of slipping and unnecessary accidents.

Types of Miters

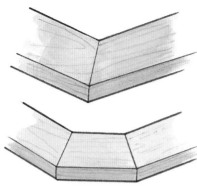

The angle of a frame miter will vary with the number of sides, but the cut is always across the width of the board face.

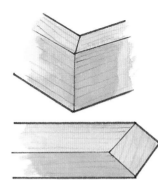

Cross miters are really bevels on the end of the board so it's not unusual to also hear them called end bevels.

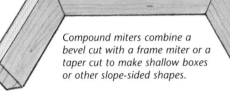

Compound miters combine a bevel cut with a frame miter or a taper cut to make shallow boxes or other slope-sided shapes.

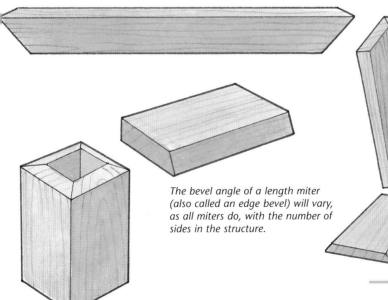

The bevel angle of a length miter (also called an edge bevel) will vary, as all miters do, with the number of sides in the structure.

Setting Up and Checking Miters

To check a 45° miter square for accuracy, align an architect's triangle to it, then hold the triangle and flip the square so any gap shows double its error.

Gap is twice the error

Align the same increment as shown above right on each framing-square leg to the miter gauge slot. Set the gauge to 45°, using longer lengths for accurate setting.

Test a 45° miter gauge setting by trimming a scrap end, flipping it for a second cut and then checking the apex of the triangular cut-off for square.

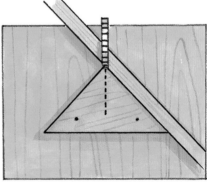

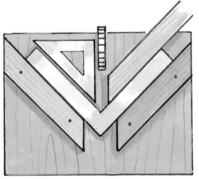

Shopmade jigs that slide in the table saw's miter gauge slots or sit fixed on the radial-arm saw table help to cut accurate miters, especially on large parts.

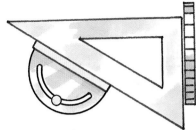

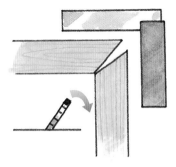

Set angles other than 45° directly from architect's triangles, or transfer the angle from a drawing to the wood's underside and set the miter gauge to it.

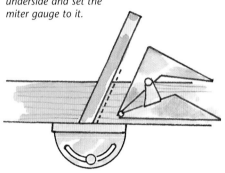

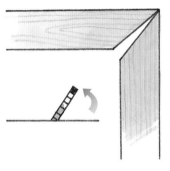

Test-fit bevels by holding parts in position against a square (or a sliding T-bevel set to a drawing for larger angles), then adjust the blade to correct the bevel.

When angles exceed the miter gauge capacity, an auxiliary fence or tapered block will extend the range of the gauge.

Using a sliding T-bevel to transfer the bevel angle from a protractor and set the blade tilt or mitering angle on a table saw or radial-arm saw.

Figuring Miters and Bevels

No other joinery employs as much mathematics as miters and bevels.

The cutting angle for frame miters and bevel joints is calculated by dividing the number of sides into a circle's 360° to find the miter angle. The cutting angle is half that. Depending on the angle or the machine's calibrations, the gauge, blade, or radial arm is set either directly to the cutting angle or to its complement (the remainder when the cutting angle is subtracted from 90°). To improve on the miter gauge's accuracy, lay out permanent settings for common angles on the table saw top using a framing square and a little geometry, first making sure the table saw blade sits parallel to the miter gauge slots.

Extend the miter fence with a straightedge to a point marked on the bisecting line, lock the setting and test the cut for accuracy with layout tools or against a careful drawing. The farther out the testing point is placed along the bisecting line, the finer the adjustments to tune the gauge setting. Punch a permanent small dent in the tabletop when the right setting is found.

Trigonometry

Trigonometry is useful for accuracy with less-common angles. Use it directly to set the miter gauge with a framing square, or to lay out an angle's rise and run on a jig or on paper to transfer to machines with layout tools. Trigonometry will also find the inside or outside length for the frame of an existing object or to fit the frame inside a defined space.

Compound miters require a combination of two settings on the radial-arm or table saw. Shown in this chapter are two drafting method to find the bevel angle and the miter or taper angle.

Miters and Math

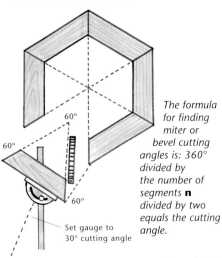

*The formula for finding miter or bevel cutting angles is: 360° divided by the number of segments **n** divided by two equals the cutting angle.*

Set gauge to 30° cutting angle

(360 ÷ n) ÷ 2 = cutting angle

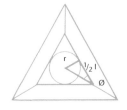

The formula to find the inside length of a concentric, equilateral shape is: Length equals twice the radius divided by the tangent of the miter angle.

l = 2r ÷ tan Ø

The formula to find the outside length of a concentric equilateral shape is: Length equals twice the radius times the cosine of the miter angle.

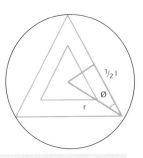

L = 2r cos Ø

Applying Geometry to Machine Set-ups

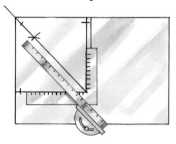

To find a 45° angle on the table saw, erect a perpendicular to the miter slot and bisect the angle, then punch a dent on the line to use to set the miter fence with a straightedge.

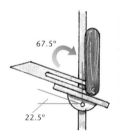

Bisecting the 45° angle above yields an accurate 22.5°; transfer any of the marked angles or complementary angles to a sliding T-bevel to set blade tilt.

Finding Angles by Drafting

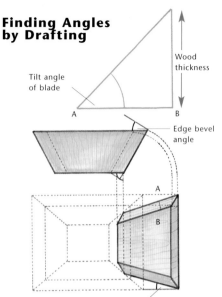

Lay a compound miter flat to see the true shape and the miter angle, then erect perpendicular AB, measure, and scale with the wood thickness to find the blade tilt.

Applying Trigonometry to Mitering

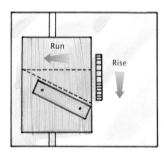

Trigonometry ratios can also be used to set the miter gauge if the increments of the rise and run on framing square legs are aligned to the miter gauge slot.

Trigonometry tables can be used to find the tangent of a desired angle and the ratio of rise to run; the points can then be marked on a sliding jig whose fence is along their hypotenuse.

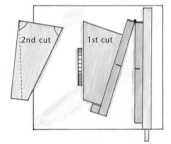

Open a taper jig's legs to the slope per foot 12" (30.5 cm) from the pivot point, rip the taper angle, then double the opening and flip the board to make the second cut.

Frame miter by hand

Miters cut across the grain with the blade perpendicular to the wood's face allow framing of panels, fields, or pictures in a flat plane. The common 45° miter makes a rectilinear shape with four sides. Six- or eight-sided shapes are also familiar and form the basis for further shaping into oval and round frames like those used as tabletop banding.

A simple frame miter is an end-grain butt joint whose only strength comes from the type of glue holding it together. A very light frame glued with epoxy might survive a low-stress application, but most frame miters need reinforcement to last.

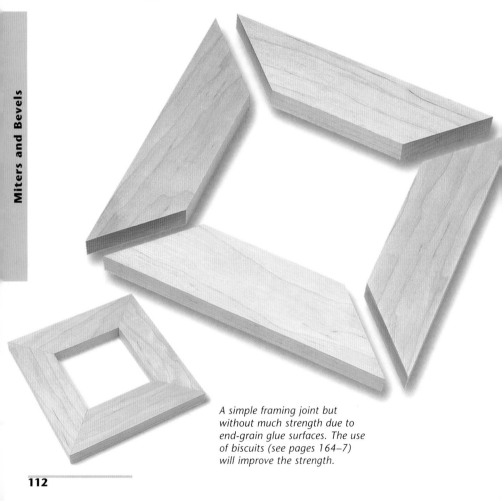

A simple framing joint but without much strength due to end-grain glue surfaces. The use of biscuits (see pages 164–7) will improve the strength.

Frame Miter by Hand

1 Mark 45° with a layout tool or scribe the diagonal of a square whose sides equal the wood width, and clamp a block there to guide the saw.

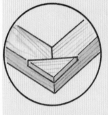

2 Lightly shave the joint of saw marks on a miter shooting board with a rabbet or other plane, shimming a playing card between the fence and part to correct misfits.

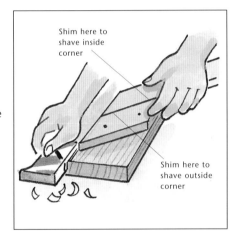

Shim here to shave inside corner

Shim here to shave outside corner

Frame Miters
Feather a miter on the table saw with the help of a fence jig, or just remove a portion of the corner's back side and glue in a reinforcing gusset. If it is preferable that the reinforcement should be concealed, use one or more biscuits—see pages 164–7.

Specialist picture-framers use a range of specially-designed press-in connectors.

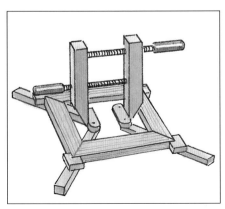

3 Heavily coat the end grain with glue. Then clamp the frame using a method like this adjustable shop made device that keeps the parts from sliding out of position when clamp force is applied.

Feathered miter on a radial-arm saw

Frame miter reinforcements are either an integral part of the joint or enhance an assembly after glue-up. Splines or joinery that create long-grain glue surfaces like the lap miter are common integral reinforcements.

Similar to the radial-arm technique shown here, a decorative hand technique for feathering frame corners is to handsaw two or three kerfs and glue contrasting veneer into them. If nails are used, drive them into the miter through the frame sides so the weight of the frame doesn't pull them out.

Using contrasting timber, in this case maple and wenge, an attractive decorative effect can be achieved.

Key

Feathered Miter on a Radial-Arm Saw

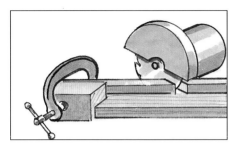

1 Set the arm to the miter angle and cut one end of each part, then clamp a stop block on the fence to exactly gauge the final cut to length.

2 Turn the saw horizontal, extending the blade about a third into the miter's length, and kerf through the frame's glued corners by sliding them into the blade on a height table.

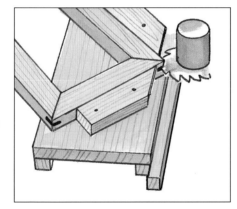

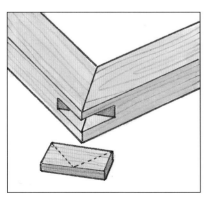

3 Thickness a strip of key material to fit the kerf and cut lengths and glue them in, then trim with a saw and sand flush after drying.

Bridle Miters A bridle miter doubles the glue surface of a lap miter when the stile is shouldered on both sides and the rail is slot-mortised and mitered to fit. This elegant reinforcement is adaptable to frames with rails and stiles of unequal thickness, and makes a stronger joint than the half-lap miter.

Lap miter

The lap miter is an elegant variation on the conventional end-lap joint (see page 45). Its merits are that it has a much greater strength than a conventional miter, and provides a "picture frame" appearance, though on the front face only. The improved strength is gained by the much-increased gluing area and the long-grain contact.

The lap miter joint can be produced accurately and quickly on a table saw using a simple shop-made sliding jig as illustrated. If the saw cuts are placed just a little proud so as to leave some material to be removed, the joint can be cleaned up with a chisel finally to achieve a perfect close fit, even with softwoods. Take particular care not to cut too deep when kerfing across the face. Too deep a cut will weaken the joint and spoil the finished appearance as well.

The use of a half lap at the rear of the miter brings a vast improvement to the glue area and hence the strength.

Lap Miter

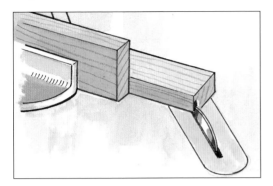

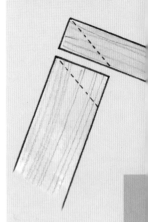

1 Cut the parts to final length and set the depth of cut to half the thickness, then kerf across the face corner of the frame stiles (the vertical parts) at 45°.

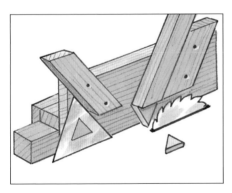

2 Use a sliding fence jig with stops at 45° to the saw table to cut away half the thickness of the kerfed corners of the stiles without touching the shoulders.

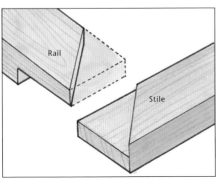

Rail

Stile

3 Cut square end laps (see page 51) on the horizontal rails, and trim the halved portion to 45° to fit against the shoulder of each stile.

Miter Angles
Mitering will accommodate frame members of different width if the miter angle is drawn on one part and transferred to the other with a sliding T-bevel.

The greater the difference between the widths of the joining parts the more difficult it is to make this joint accurately and the weaker it becomes. Not recommended if the difference is greater than two-to-one.

Housed rabbet miter

Cross miters made by bevel cuts across the grain are, like frame miters, inherently weak joints because of their end-grain glue surface. Fortunately, also like frame miters, they are used more in supplemental rather than structural capacities. Most of the reinforcing techniques that are used on frame miters also apply to cross miters, but the decorative butterfly key is eliminated and replaced by the dovetail key (see page 146), which makes mock dovetails for the cross miter.

The housed rabbet miter adds no long-grain glue surface to a cross miter joint. Its slight shoulder adds a little glue shearing strength and some assistance against racking, but real strength comes from pins driven through the joint from the outside or from making the joint long-grain.

This elegant joint originates in Japan. Use pins made of a contrasting wood for decorative effect.

Shop-turned pins

Housed Rabbet Miter

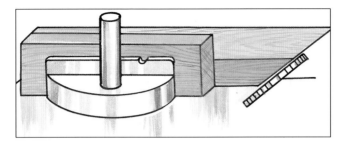

1 Using material that is the same thickness as its mating corner (or thinner like this drawer side), bevel the end to 45°.

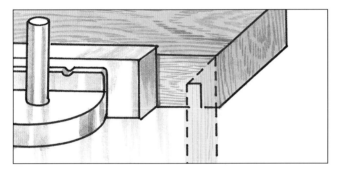

2 Cut the drawer front to length and kerf across its inside face within an outline of the side's thickness and just to half the height of its bevel.

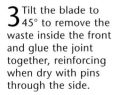

3 Tilt the blade to 45° to remove the waste inside the front and glue the joint together, reinforcing when dry with pins through the side.

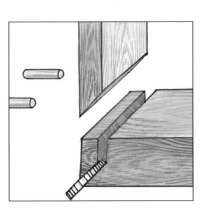

VARIATIONS

Stop block sets miter gauge cut

Reinforcing Cross Miters Leave the blade at 45° to kerf for splines in the outer three-quarters of the end-grain glue surface of 45° cross miters.

Other Degrees Cross miters at other than 45° are dadoed on end on the router table or table saw with the blade square and the bevel riding flat on the table.

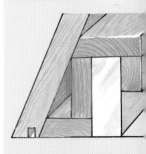

Locked miter

With end grain to end grain in an L orientation, a cross miter is hard to modify for long-grain contact except by combining it with the finger joint (shown on page 55). Even internal splines don't make long-grain contact unless the joint is part of a six- or eight-sided structure where the joint angle is greater than 120°. Feathering through the corners does bring long-grain strength to cross miters.

The tablesawn locked-miter joint shown here automatically interlocks the joint so it depends less on glue strength, but it's only effective when it's correctly oriented to resist tension. Locked miters are a common joint for drawers because they're strong against pulling on the drawer front and show no end grain on the front or side.

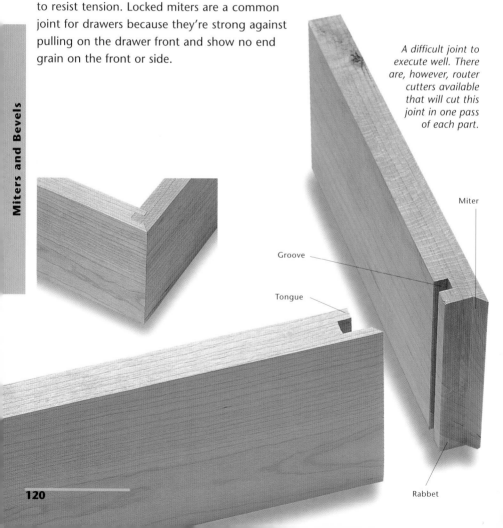

A difficult joint to execute well. There are, however, router cutters available that will cut this joint in one pass of each part.

Miter

Groove

Tongue

Rabbet

Locked Miter

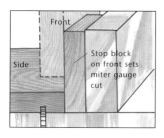

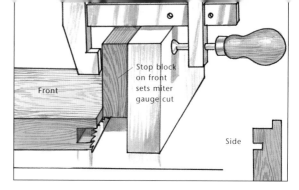

1 Set the blade in line with the front thickness. Kerf on the inside face of the side with the blade height about a third of the side's thickness.

4 Use a normal blade lowered to cut only the narrow tongue in the front, trimming it to the depth of the dado kerfed a third into the side thickness.

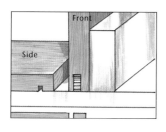

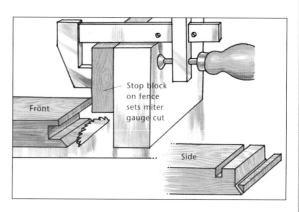

2 Dado to the height of the side thickness at a width about half the front thickness, leaving a narrow tongue to fit the side's kerf.

5 Tilt the blade to 45° and use a stop block on the fence to control the beveling of projecting tongues on the front and side.

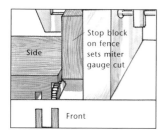

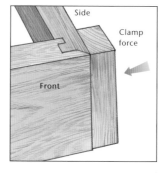

3 Set a stop block, lower the dado blade to two-thirds the thickness, then cut a rabbet that leaves a tongue to fit the dado in the front.

6 Unlike most miters, a locked miter needs clamp force to be applied in only one direction, but a block should distribute pressure on the miter itself.

Waterfall joint

A plain bevel joint along the grain brings an air of harmony to joinery, because the joint line blends so well with the material that the parts merge into a single unit. Length miters (or bevel joints) also bring with them a world of segmented joinery populated by umbrella stands, planters, and kaleidoscopes. Length miters have grain orientation that is strong for gluing once the parts co-operate with clamping.

The waterfall joint capitalizes on a miter's ability to carry the grain around a turn. It's particularly good in custom veneered plywood cabinets where the back is seen. The back is taken from the center of the sheet, the ends jointed to it by a waterfall, and the face frame attached.

Miters and Bevels

The name "waterfall" joint derives from the fact that the grain pattern tumbles down over the right-angled joint.

Waterfall Joint

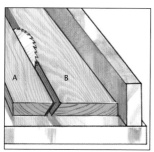

1 Tilt the blade to 45° and rip a bevel with the outer face up for a tilt toward the fence or the inside face up for an outward tilt.

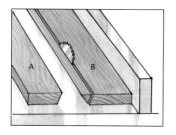

2 Flip end for end the piece that is against the fence and rip again to remove a triangular waste strip from the wood's edge.

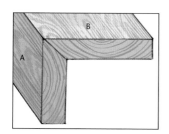

3 Flip the fence piece back again and join to the first piece to achieve a near-perfect grain match.

Segments
Segmented constructions are easier to glue in pairs so the bevel joint makes full contact along its entire length.

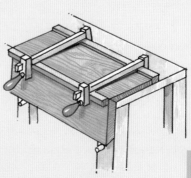

Angled fingerboards
Groove bevels at 45° using their cutting tilt for the blade angle setting, and clamp down an angled fingerboard, kerfed until it's flexible to hold the part vertical against the fence.

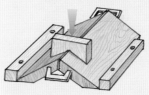

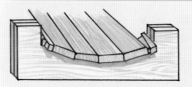

Coopering This technique uses bevel-modified width joints to join segments of a circle's arc into one unit that may be turned over and planed smooth of facets after the glue dries.

Rabbet miter

Length miters have a long glue line and the bevel angle will slip under pressure. Splines (page 29) or biscuits (page 164) stop the slipping, but it is still difficult to keep the joint from opening up on the inside or outside if clamp force is misdirected. When the construction has more than the four segments found in box shapes, gluing up bevel joints is easier to do in stages, two parts at a time.

A self-squaring joint like the rabbet miter, with its inside step to butt the miters and keep the joint in position, is a helpful choice for square structures. Still, the outside corner of the miter benefits from the corner clamping blocks to press it tight. This joint is possible on a router table with a straight bit and a chamfering bit.

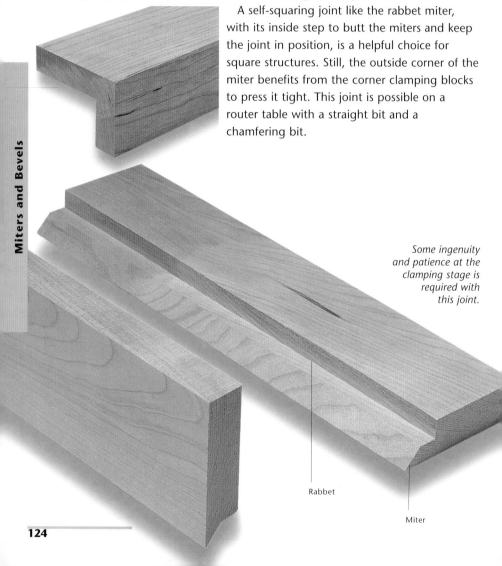

Some ingenuity and patience at the clamping stage is required with this joint.

Rabbet

Miter

Rabbet Miter

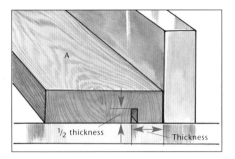

1 Kerf the inside face with the distance between the fence and the *outside* of the blade equal to the wood thickness and the blade height set to half the thickness.

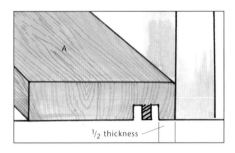

2 Move the fence so the distance to the blade's *inside* is half the wood thickness and kerf again, then move the fence to waste the material between the kerfs.

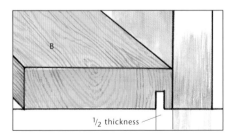

3 Without changing the blade height, move the fence back so the distance to the blade's *outside* is half the thickness and kerf the inside face of the second part.

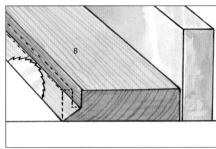

4 Flip the second part end for end so the inside is up, and tilt the blade to remove the waste to the kerf at a 45° angle.

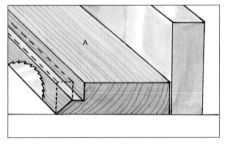

5 Flip the first part inside up and bevel its edge at the same 45° bevel angle, cutting to the groove left by kerfing out the waste.

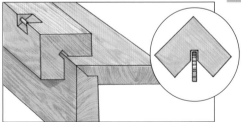

6 Make two cuts in a long wood square to waste out a corner and kerf inside the clamping block's angle to keep glue squeeze from sticking it to the miter.

Compound miter by machine

Combining a miter angle with a blade tilt creates a compound miter. These miters tilt the sides of boxes and stave constructions outward or inward. If the slope angle (the degree of tilt out or in) isn't critical, a "ball park" miter angle and blade tilt will make an object that fits together.

The table saw or radial-arm saw makes quick work of compound cutting once the set-up is tested in scraps. Like any miter, accuracy is critical. An error of one degree on each cut will multiply with the number of sides until the object won't fit together. One or two slight misalignments at glue-up will throw off the joinery

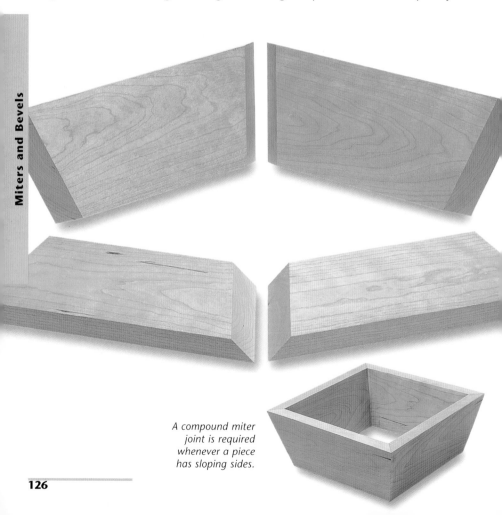

A compound miter joint is required whenever a piece has sloping sides.

Compound Miter by Machine

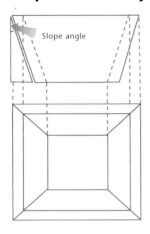

Slope angle

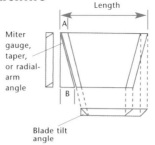

Length

A

Miter gauge, taper, or radial-arm angle

B

Blade tilt angle

3 Project from the side view and use measurements A and B to lay out the miter angle, extending this angle's line and parallels to find the tilt angle.

1 Draw a full-size elevation at the intended slope angle and develop a plan view of the piece.

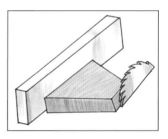

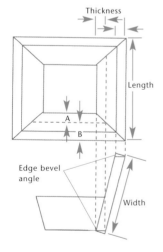

Thickness

Length

A
B

Edge bevel angle

Width

2 Drop perpendiculars from the plan and lay out the slope angle across them to find the actual part width and the edge bevel angle so the piece sits flat.

4 Set blade and gauge angles and miter one end of all parts, then tilt the gauge oppositely, turn the other edge to the gauge fence and cut to final length.

5 Cut the edge bevel on the top and bottom so the piece will sit flat, shifting the fence if necessary so the miter's point doesn't slip under it.

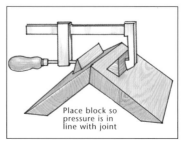

Place block so pressure is in line with joint

6 Temporarily glue beveled strips with paper between for easy removal to direct the clamp force to the joint. Glue the piece in sections.

Compound miter by hand

A plan and elevation of any project should be drawn to work out problems before cutting begins. But neither view of a splayed object shows the actual shape of its parts or the actual miter and blade tilt angles.

Compound miters are not impossible by hand, but they may not be practical with many sides or segments. The success of handmade compound miters depends on skill with a hand plane.

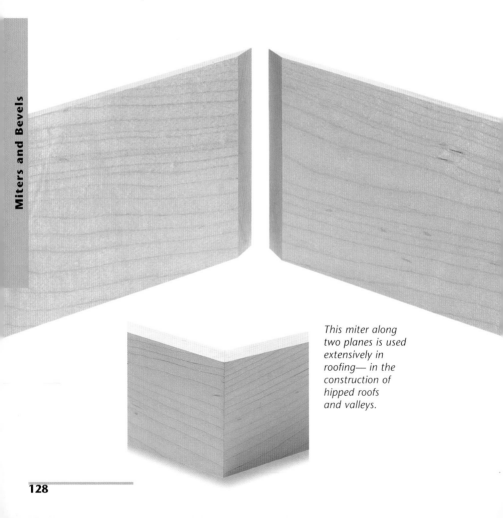

This miter along two planes is used extensively in roofing— in the construction of hipped roofs and valleys.

Compound Miter by Hand

Coping and Mitering Moulding

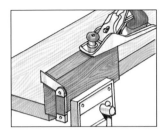

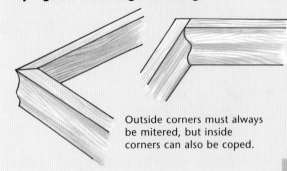

1 Use the drawing methods on page 127 to find the bevel angle, mark it on each end of a guide block and plane the edge to it.

Outside corners must always be mitered, but inside corners can also be coped.

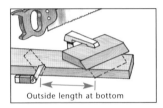

Outside length at bottom

A moulding that overhangs itself can only be mitered.

A moulding that generally sweeps back can be coped.

2 Clamp the saw guide block across the inside of the part at the miter angle, making sure the bevel guides the saw cut toward the outside length of the part.

Cope saw profile

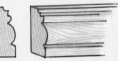

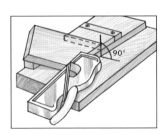

To cope a moulding, bevel across the face to show the profile line, then cope saw along the profile vertically or slightly undercut and sand or file to fit.

3 On a shooting board, use double-stick tape to hold a tapered fence block that aligns the miter and a wood strip that tilts the bevel to 90°. Shave the miters to fit.

To cut a crown moulding, mark the cabinet width on the moulding bottom and align to the miter slot, propping the moulding upside down and flat against the fence to cut the miter.

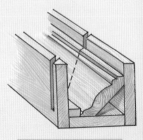

CHOOSING AND USING DOVETAILS

The classic handmade through dovetail joint is very strong—and not as difficult to make as it may look.

Often considered the hallmark of fine workmanship in wood, dovetails are an interlocking joint with a great deal of mechanical strength. The joint is constructed with an angled male part shaped like the joint's name which fits into a similarly shaped female socket. In its best-known configuration at an end-to-end face corner, a dovetail joint is a series of tails fitting into a series of sockets.

The parts between sockets are called pins. They fit like interlocking tenons into the spaces between the tails. The widening tail braces the joint against tension, adding great mechanical strength to the long-grain glue surface between the tails and pins.

The three basic dovetail corner joints are through, half-blind or lapped, and blind or double lapped. The type to use depends on the furniture style and on strength requirements. In antique furniture, the strongest through dovetails (whose ends break through the board's face) were hidden under mouldings. Half-blind or blind dovetails also kept the dovetail ends or entire joint from showing. Contemporary designs feature through dovetails on the carcass corners and drawers to advertise handcrafting. Modern adjustable dovetailing jigs imitate handwork, yielding variably spaced dovetails that subject this "handcrafted" look to scrutiny.

The dovetail shape transforms other joint families to strengthen them against tension. The sliding dovetail modifies a male tongue or tenon to fit a matching female housing. In the lap joint family, end laps reshaped as dovetails are used to relieve tension on the glue bond, and end edge laps can include dovetailed shoulders that hold their unsupported end grain.

Modification of laps and sliding tongues and tenons has two forms: a single dovetail is barefaced with only one angled side and shoulder; a double dovetail has the full dovetail shape and usually includes a shoulder on each side.

Dovetail splines are used like regular splines to join wood. The butterfly key and the dovetail key are decorative, functional reinforcing devices let into mating sockets.

Dovetail Terminology

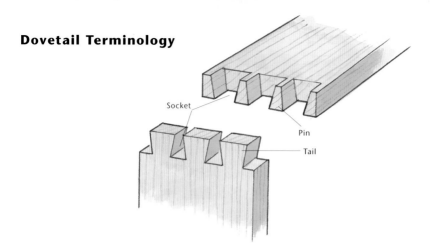

Socket

Pin

Tail

Basic Corner Dovetails

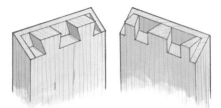

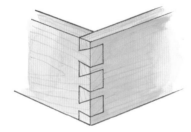

Through dovetails yield the largest glue surface possible in the joint, but the ends of the boards show through on the mating faces.

A blind mitered dovetail joint gives a corner joint hidden strength but allows the visual continuation of unbroken grain around the assembly.

Half-blind dovetails hold a drawer face to the sides without letting the board ends show through on the drawer front.

On blind dovetails, the tails aren't cut through both faces like half-blind dovetails, and either the pins or tails lap to keep any hint of dovetails from view.

Decorative Dovetail Reinforcements

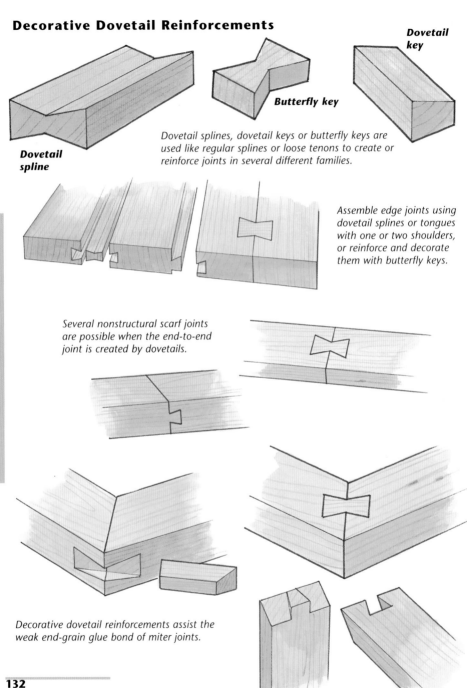

Dovetail key

Butterfly key

Dovetail spline

Dovetail splines, dovetail keys or butterfly keys are used like regular splines or loose tenons to create or reinforce joints in several different families.

Assemble edge joints using dovetail splines or tongues with one or two shoulders, or reinforce and decorate them with butterfly keys.

Several nonstructural scarf joints are possible when the end-to-end joint is created by dovetails.

Decorative dovetail reinforcements assist the weak end-grain glue bond of miter joints.

Dovetails

Modifying Joints with Dovetails

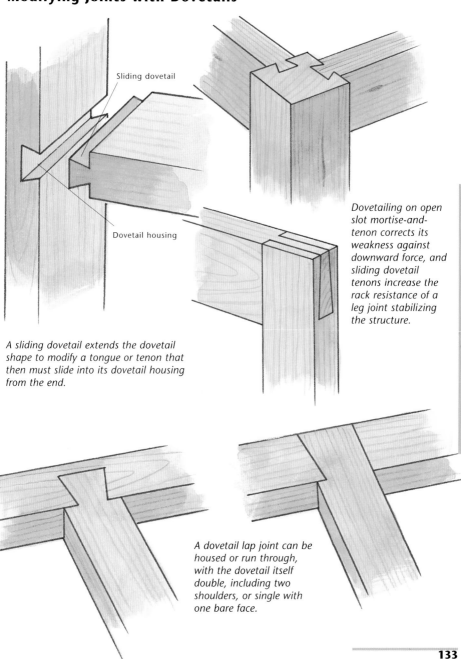

Sliding dovetail

Dovetail housing

Dovetailing on open slot mortise-and-tenon corrects its weakness against downward force, and sliding dovetail tenons increase the rack resistance of a leg joint stabilizing the structure.

A sliding dovetail extends the dovetail shape to modify a tongue or tenon that then must slide into its dovetail housing from the end.

A dovetail lap joint can be housed or run through, with the dovetail itself double, including two shoulders, or single with one bare face.

Through dovetail

When developing a corner dovetail layout, make the pins about half the wood's thickness (or more at their widest) and make the evenly spaced tails about two or three times the pin width.

Variable spacing uses wide tails at the center and narrower tails toward the joint's ends, setting out more pin gluing surface there but not necessarily proportioning the pins to either tail. This places strong construction where it's needed and helps restrain cupping if the wood dries. Layout should orient the heartwood outside to compensate for drying—drawers will bind if the sides cup outward.

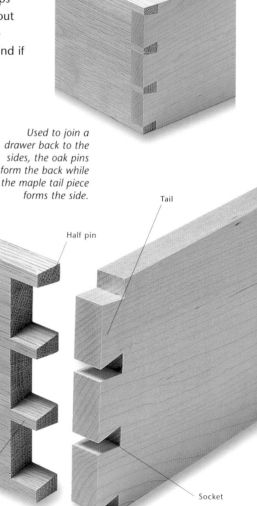

Used to join a drawer back to the sides, the oak pins form the back while the maple tail piece forms the side.

Half pin

Tail

Pin

Socket

Through Pins

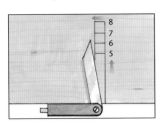

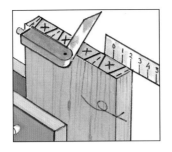

1 Considering the type and species of wood, butt a sliding T-bevel to the bench edge and set the dovetail angle to a ratio between 1:5 and 1:8.

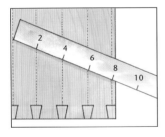

2 Design the layout on paper to develop sizes; tilting a ruler diagonally is an easy way to set equal increments for the pin center lines and the spaces for mating tails.

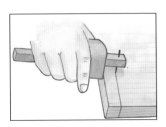

3 Dress and sand the wood, set the marking gauge just over the tail part's thickness. Scribe around the end of the pin piece for faces and edges.

4 Facing the board's inside, lay out the pin center lines, mark half the pin's widest end on each side of the center line, scribe the angles with a knife, and mark the waste.

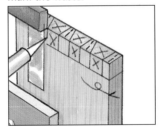

5 Square the pin angles down each face of the board to the gauged line with a knife and clearly mark the waste.

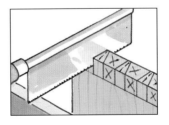

6 Starting at the front corner on the waste side of the pin lines, saw part way on the face and end, then level out to saw to the gauged line.

Through Dovetail

TRADE SECRETS

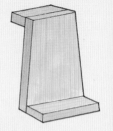

Simple Jigs A piece of scrap cut at the dovetail angle with attached stops at each end aids marking and guarantees the angle will stay the same.

Table saw Pins Saw pins on the table saw with the blade lowered to the gauged line and the miter gauge angled to align the cut to the dovetail angle.

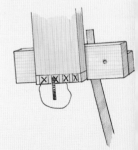

135

TRADE SECRETS

Bandsaw Pins To saw pins on the bandsaw, tilt the bandsaw table itself or make a tilted jig, using a clamped block to stop the cut at the gauged line.

Layout Tools A homemade layout tool for dovetails can set the angle for the tails and pins, as well as square the lines across the end grain and down the face.

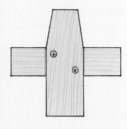

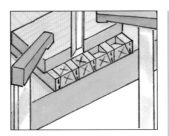

7 Clamp the part over a bench leg with a guide block on the gauged line, chop down at the line and chisel away half the waste, angling down from the end grain.

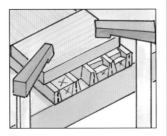

8 Flip the part and chop away the remaining waste with small steps that move back toward the gauged line and down into the waste until all the waste is removed.

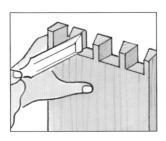

9 Clean up inside the pins, making sure to keep the cheeks flat and perpendicular, and pare the end grain flat or undercut to a slight V indent.

Through Tails

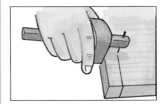

1 Set the marking gauge slightly over the thickness of the pin stock and scribe around the end of the tail stock after it has been dressed, squared, and sanded.

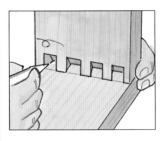

2 Hold or clamp the widest side of the cut pins to the gauged line on the tails, scribing inside the sockets to mark the pin positions inside the tail stock.

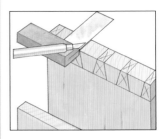

3 Square the scribed pin angle lines across the end of the board and mark the pin positions as waste.

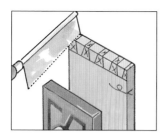

4 Saw on the waste side of the pin angles, starting on the front corner to saw face and end simultaneously, tilting the board to make the cuts vertical if preferred.

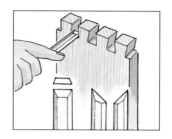

7 Clean up the sockets between the tails, using if necessary special skew or dovetail chisels with angled edges that can reach under the overhang of the tail.

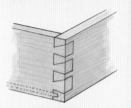

Drawer Dovetails
The layout of through dovetails on drawers allows the bottom groove to run out under a tail and through a pin where the open groove on the drawer's side is plugged.

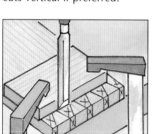

5 One method chops out the waste with a narrow chisel using the same process as with the pins, tilting the chisel slightly if undercut end grain is desired.

8 Protect the joint with a block and tap it together, making sure that the pins and tails align to their sockets and that their wide ends aren't too tight and cause splits.

Miter Layouts
A corner miter dovetail layout insets the half pin from the edge, but one face line of the half pin isn't sawn, and the extra material beyond it is mitered.

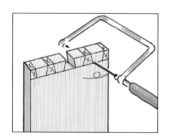

6 Another method removes the waste by sawing near the line, then paring the end grain flush to the gauge line.

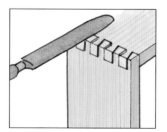

9 After gluing, file or use a block to sand flush the raised pins and tails caused by gauging the line a little over the thickness of the stock.

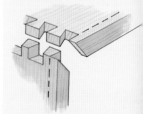

Through Dovetail

137

Half-blind dovetail

The biggest difference from through dovetails is that lapped dovetails, such as half-blind or blind mitered, help to hide all or part of the joint to serve design. Half-blind dovetails use two gauge settings for layout regardless of part thickness, while through dovetails can use the same setting for all gauging unless part thickness differs. When laying out half-blinds, the scribe on the end grain not only sets the length of the tails but it establishes the joint's strength based on glue surface and mechanical resistance. Never under-scribe this dimension onto the tails part or misalign the tails to it for scribing, or the joint won't fit tight.

A half-blind or blind dovetail is used to join the front of the drawer to the sides leaving a plain drawer front still utilizing the great strength of dovetails.

Drawer front

Socket

Drawer side

Tail

Half pin

Half-Blind Dovetail

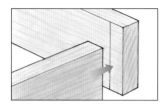

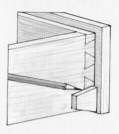

1 Using a drawer as the example, square and sand the stock, set the marking gauge to the side's thickness, and then scribe it on the inside face of the front.

4 After sawing and chiseling the tails, hold the parts in the assembly position; with the tails exactly on the front's end-grain scribe line to scribe them on to the front's end.

Lipped Drawers
The sides are dovetailed into the rabbet cut around the edge of the drawer front, and pins are marked from a template or from tails made first.

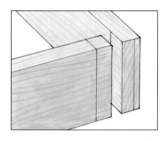

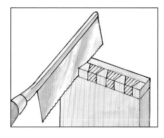

2 Reset the gauge to scribe about two-thirds thickness of the front on its end grain and also around the end of the side on both the faces and edges.

5 Mark the tails scribed on the front's end as waste, and saw tilted from the front corner until the kerf reaches both scribed lines but doesn't go past them.

Runner Grooves
When using half-blind dovetails, lay out the runner groove of side-hung draws so it uses the drawer front as a stop.

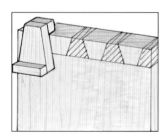

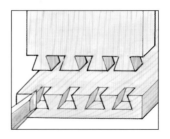

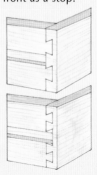

3 Determine the layout spacing and sizes and use a template or sliding bevel to scribe angles for the tails on the side's outside face. Square the lines across the end.

6 Chop down into the waste and chip it out from the end grain, guide the chisel against the pin side to reach the unsawn inside corners, then test fit the joint.

Blind mitered dovetail

Initially, the tail and pin parts of blind mitered dovetails are laid out the same as for half-blind ones. Equally thick parts are rabbeted from the inside face about two-thirds the thickness toward the opposite face and about a third the distance down to the inside scribed line.

The rabbet width and depth should intersect at a point along the 45° shoulder line scribed on the part's edge. Then the pins are laid out on the rabbet like a mitered corner dovetail, and the tails are scribed from them.

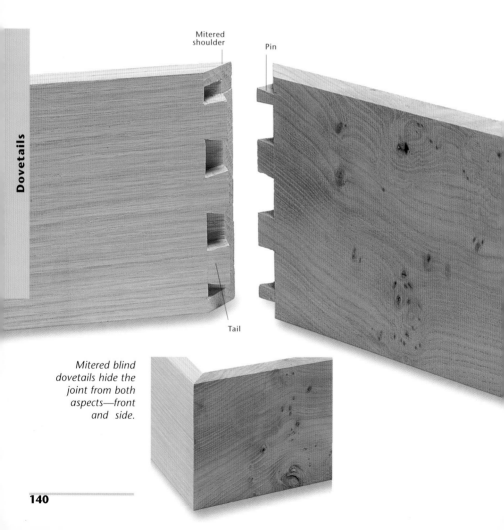

Mitered shoulder

Pin

Tail

Mitered blind dovetails hide the joint from both aspects—front and side.

Blind Mitered Dovetail

1 Scribe the exact thickness inside each part, connect a 45° scribe from each edge, then rabbet about a third toward the face scribe but not past the angled line.

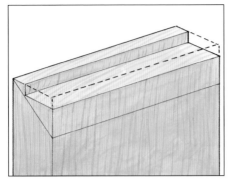

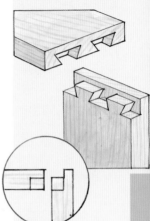

2 Lay out the pins with a template, leaving material past the half pin as in mitered corner dovetails. Clear the sockets, saw the edge's mitered shoulder, and finally miter the end lip.

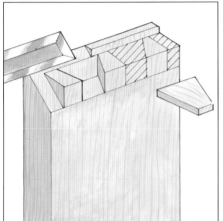

Full-Blind Dovetails These are similar to half-blind and blind mitered dovetails, with either the pins or tails carrying the lap and the layout keeping the joint hidden from view. If one part is to be load bearing, that part must carry the pins.

3 Place the pin part in position on the tail part against the scribed lines, scribe the tails, remove the socket waste, and cut the mitered shoulder and mitered end.

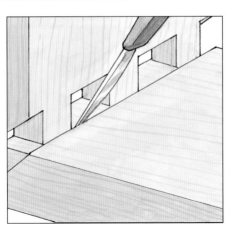

Blind Mitred Dovetail

Stopped tapered dovetail by hand

The sliding dovetail is a modification that mechanically reinforces certain tongues or tenons against tension. The oldest hand-cut versions like the tapered sliding dovetail, a housing joint, are being replaced by routed versions, often without the taper. These have the liability of being more difficult to slide over a length than the tapered version, which begins to tighten only as the last few inches are slid home.

There are as many methods for routing sliding dovetails as there are woodworkers, but no matter how the joint is made, material flatness affects accurate milling and in turn the ease of assembly.

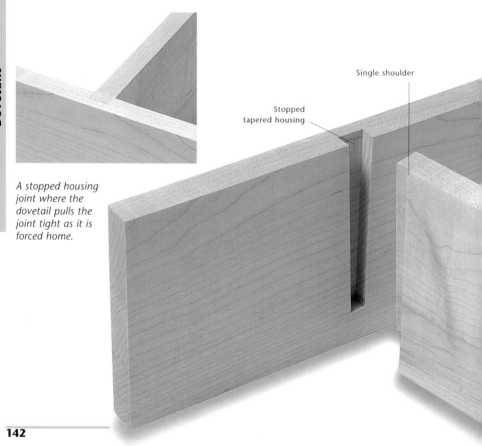

A stopped housing joint where the dovetail pulls the joint tight as it is forced home.

Single shoulder

Stopped tapered housing

Stopped Tapered Dovetail by Hand

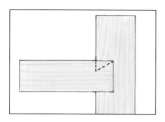

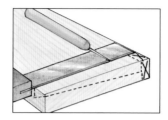

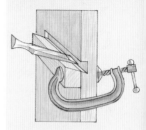

1 Match a dovetail angle to the dovetail saw and plane, then determine the width of dovetail that will fit within the stock thickness, leaving a small shoulder.

4 Scribe the dovetail depth square across the shelf face, mark the dovetail profile on the back edge, then mark the same taper angle across the end as the housing.

Guide Blocks
Make dovetail housings without special tools by ripping or planing the dovetail angle into a guide block to set the angle for chiseling and sawing the housing and tongue.

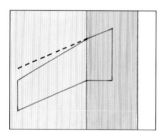

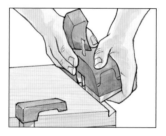

2 Lay out the dovetail width at less than half the thickness of the housing part's back edge and square lines across, but taper the top line narrower toward the front.

5 Use the dovetail plane to remove the shoulder material and taper the dovetail tongue to the marked end grain.

Routing Housings
A routed version of a dovetailed housing uses a saddle jig to guide a dado, then changes to a dovetail bit to dovetail the housing's front end either through or stopped.

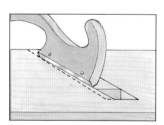

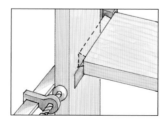

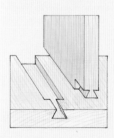

3 As in other stopped housings, chisel a hole to allow sawing, saw the straight shoulder to the correct depth, then use the angled dovetail saw to cut the shoulder.

6 Trim the tongue to the stop and test slide it into the housing, where it will be loose until the last, when a clamp can pull it tight.

Sliding dovetail drawer joint

Some classic designs used the sliding dovetail to join the drawer sides and back. The sides traditionally extended past the back to keep the drawer from falling out when fully open, and so the sliding dovetail wasn't weakened with a housing too close to the end, creating weak short grain. The dovetail held the sides in against the weight of bulging contents and the forces of drying wood. The drawer front layout needs a lip at each end so that the dovetail housing run in it isn't weakened by short grain.

Clamps help pull together long sliding dovetails, which, when used on shelving, needn't be glued their full length. Gluing at the front edge to hold the part in position is usually enough.

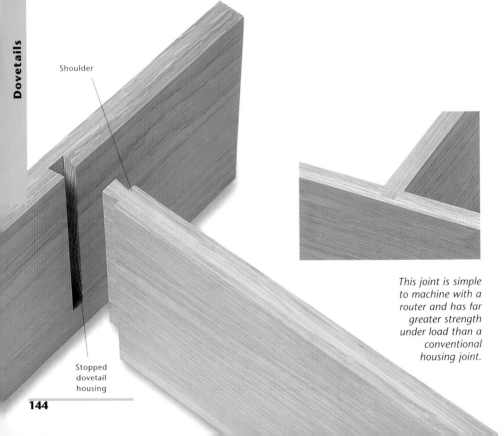

Shoulder

Stopped dovetail housing

This joint is simple to machine with a router and has far greater strength under load than a conventional housing joint.

Sliding Dovetail Drawer Joint

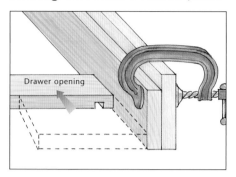

1 On a router table with an auxiliary wooden fence, steady the drawer with a plywood square and use a straight bit to waste a groove about half the material's depth.

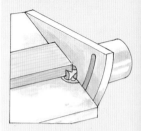

Routing Tongues
Rout tongues horizontally with a router mounted on a pivoting fence, which is locked by a knob to the table's edge so the bit can be raised to cut a second shoulder.

2 For a single shoulder dovetail, change to a dovetail bit and cut the angled shoulder without the bit touching the straight outside shoulder.

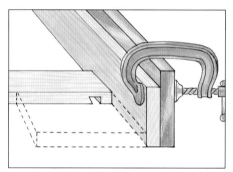

Traditionally, the sides of a drawer extending beyond the back were cut with a tapering top edge to allow the drawer to sag downward a little when fully open. Use a piece of scrap cut to the depth of the drawer sides to judge the ideal angle of the taper.

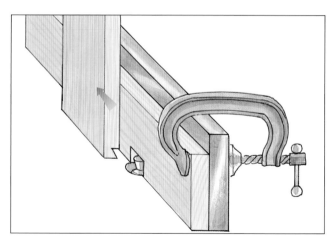

3 Without changing the bit height, slide the fence over so only part of the bit shaves the tongue on the end of drawer side until it fits the dovetail housing.

Sliding Dovetail Drawer Joint

Dovetail keys

The dovetail shape in the form of keys, splines, and butterfly keys is popular and effective as a decorative reinforcement. The butterfly key has even become the signature reinforcement of certain craft movements and craft builders.

For strength, dovetail keys are cut with the grain. One use creates mock dovetails that reinforce corner miter joints. Keys can be of a contrasting wood, but even the same species yields a color change because the trimmed key shows all end grain.

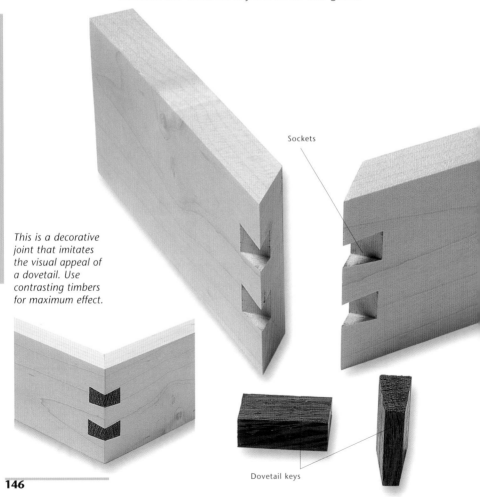

This is a decorative joint that imitates the visual appeal of a dovetail. Use contrasting timbers for maximum effect.

Sockets

Dovetail keys

Dovetail Keys

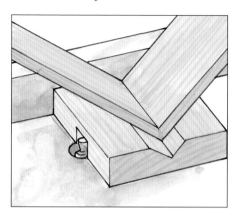

1 Rout dovetail housings in mitered corners using a V-block with a through dado for bit passage. Rout one dovetail then turn the work round to rout the other.

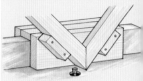

Sliding Fence Jigs
Slowly rout the corners of frames for dovetail keys with a sliding fence jig that has two stops placed at 45° to hold the frame in routing position. If the two parts of the frame are long it is advisable to fix them together with two battens pinned to them temporarily to ensure a well-fitting joint.

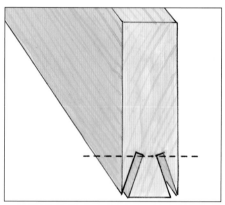

2 Set the table saw blade to the dovetail angle and make two kerfs in the edge with the grain in order to create a matching dovetail shape. Rip off the key.

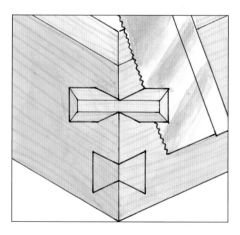

3 Tap short lengths of key material into the dovetail housing with glue, trim off with a saw once dry, and then sand.

Dovetail Keys

Butterfly keys

Butterfly keys are made so the grain runs parallel to the length of their face. Set in across the grain, they create a minor dimensional conflict to consider when designing their length. Their thickness can vary in proportion to the ground wood, the wood into which they're set.

To save chiseling recesses, make a router template in two parts for easy access to sawing the shape. Medium density fiberboard, or MDF, makes excellent template material. A flush-trim over-bearing bit eliminates the calculation of template guide offsets so the template can be cut from the scribed size of the key. The router leaves round corners to chisel out of the recess, or the key corners can be rounded instead.

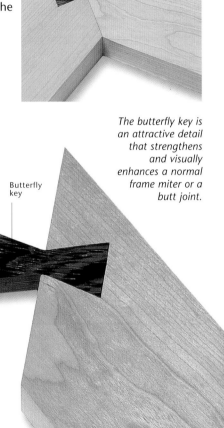

Recess

Butterfly key

The butterfly key is an attractive detail that strengthens and visually enhances a normal frame miter or a butt joint.

Butterfly Keys

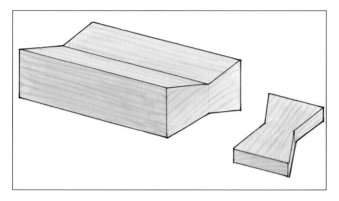

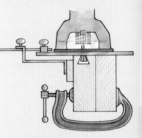

1 Make a length of dovetail spline, then cut butterfly key inlays like breads slices about a third the stock thickness being inlaid plus extra to plane flush after gluing.

Supporting Routers Rout dovetail housings or even tongues in edges and ends by clamping on extra material to support the router and aligning the cut with the router edge guide. The cut must be worked through; it is impossible to plunge a dovetail router bit. Also, the router depth-of-cut setting must be fixed. By setting a stop, the housing can be "stopped" at one end.

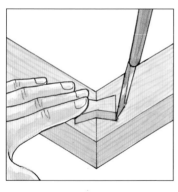

2 Hold or clamp the reinforcing inlay in place across the joint and scribe around it, tilting the knife handle away from the inlay, so the tip bevels in toward it.

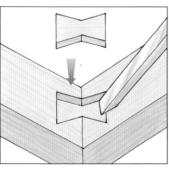

3 Chop the outline deeper in each part separately and leverage the waste with the chisel's bevel side down. Glue in the inlay, beveling its entry wedge if necessary, and plane flush when dry.

Dovetail splines

The common dovetail spline is just as easy (or difficult) to fit as a machined sliding dovetail. The housings are simple, but fitting the dovetail to it requires a lot of testing in scrap. Once the machine set-up of the router or table saw is fine-tuned, running the splines is easy. As with other splines, the grain runs across the width of dovetail splines for strength. If cut on the table saw, the V in the center of the spline might need some clean-up with a chisel or rabbet plane.

The sliding dovetail batten is a utilitarian key, made wide and fit unglued into a dovetail housing on one end of slab glue-ups such as tabletops or doors. These battens allow the wood to move but keep the assembly flat.

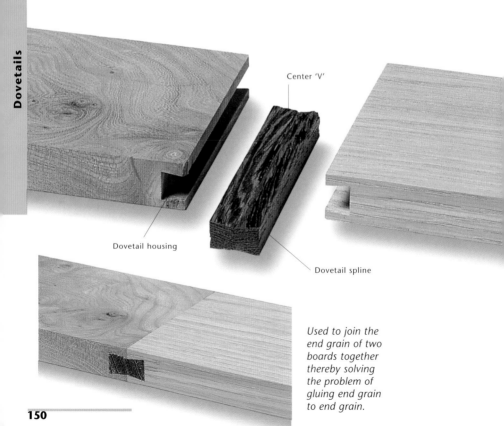

Center 'V'

Dovetail housing

Dovetail spline

Used to join the end grain of two boards together thereby solving the problem of gluing end grain to end grain.

Dovetail Splines

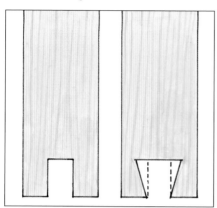

1 On a router table or table saw, make a groove to waste some of the material, then rout with a dovetail bit to form the housing.

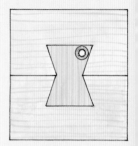

2 Lay out dovetails on a board's edge to match the housing and adjust the saw blade angle and depth. The cut the first two angles, rotate end for end, and cut the others.

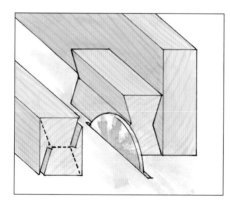

Dovetail Splines

Cutting Recesses
Butt two pieces of template material, outline a butterfly key, separate them to saw interior angles, then glue together to guide a flush-trim over-bearing bit to rout the recess.

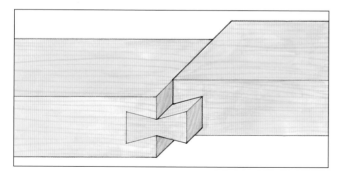

3 Test the spline's fit, thinning it slightly with a rabbet plane or sanding block if it's too tight, then tap the parts together or pull together with a clamp.

About dowels

Dowels, or dowel pins, are cylindrical bits of wood that form a joint when glued like loose tenons into aligning holes drilled in two wood parts. Their basic functions in joinery are to substitute for tenons and tongues, or to reinforce or to align joints.

Commercial birch or maple dowels come in standard diameters from ¼" (0.6 cm) to ½" (1.25 cm) and several lengths. Alternatively dowels can be made in the shop from lengths of dowel rod. Chamfered dowel ends ease insertion and keep dowels from burring over when they're tapped home. Tapping in the dowel can create a piston effect, compressing air and glue in the hole. This hydraulic pressure makes assembly difficult and could split the part. To relieve the pressure, spiral or straight flutes are cut in the dowels. In use, dowel diameter should be a third to half the part thickness. Holes in each part should be drilled to a minimum depth of one and a half times the diameter, and countersunk to collect escaping glue. Commercial dowels must be kept dry so they don't swell with moisture. Swollen dowels can be dried in an oven before use.

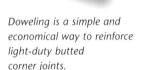

Doweling is a simple and economical way to reinforce light-duty butted corner joints.

Making dowels

Shop-made dowels are cut from doweling rod sized by driving it through a dowel plate, a piece of mild steel drilled with the appropriate size hole, and countersinking on the exiting side. The rod can be fluted and cut to lengths or each cut length can be fluted and chamfered for insertion.

Strength

The quality and durability of dowel joints are widely debated. While they might not substitute for dovetails, with extra design flexibility, dowels in a wall-hung cabinet have the same chance as any other joint to endure the stresses of wood movement on the glue bond.

Because dowels are wood they are subject to the same effects of wood movements on length and width as any other wood part. Depending on grain orientation, a dowel joint will be strong and free from dimensional conflict, or it will have little long-grain contact for gluing, lots of conflict, and be weak against tensions and glue shear.

Dowelmaking in the Shop

Dowel rod is sized by driving it through holes in a steel dowel plate or pop; holes in commercial versions are sometimes toothed inside to simultaneously cut flutes.

Another way to add flutes to dowels cut from rod is to run them along a saw blade to form one or two glue channels.

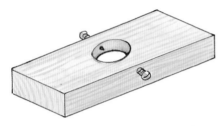

A cheap and effective fluter can be made from scrap wood with a hole that fits a dowel rod; screw or nail points protruding into the hole cut the flutes.

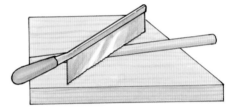

Some woodworkers roll dowel rod with a saw held on the diagonal to make teeth marks that hold dried glue like flutes, theorizing that it mechanically reinforces the glue bond.

Types of Dowels

Commercial spiral-fluted dowels allow excess glue and air to escape from the hole, avoiding hydraulic pressure as the joint is assembled. Straight-fluted commercial dowels don't scrape all the glue off the sides of the hole and are easy to insert, but they are not as readily available.

A dowel pointer chucks into a drill or brace and works like a pencil sharpener to chamfer dowel ends, or twirl the ends against a belt or disk sander.

153

Precision Doweling

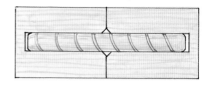

A countersink enlarges the dowel hole, making a reservoir to contain escaping glue that would otherwise ooze out onto the wood surface.

Dowel holes should be drilled a minimum of one and a half times the diameter in each part, with a slight glue reservoir at the bottom and at the countersunk edge.

Dowels and Wood Movement

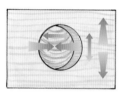 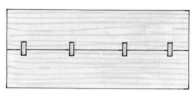

In the worst grain orientation, a dowel will shrink away from the mostly end-grain glue surface in its hole and subject the joint to racking.

The long grain of dowels in width joints creates dimensional conflict against width movement; dowels should be cut under length and spaced widely if used for alignment in such situations.

In a length joint, the long grain of dowels runs parallel to that of the parts, so there is no conflict.

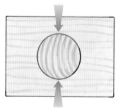

Even inserted in the best orientation where the dowel moves in the same direction as the part's wood, a dowel has only two tiny points of long-grain contact with its hole.

In certain corner applications, dowels create dimensional conflicts similar to pinned mortise-and-tenon joints, but other doweled corners present little conflict and offer design opportunities not possible with other joints.

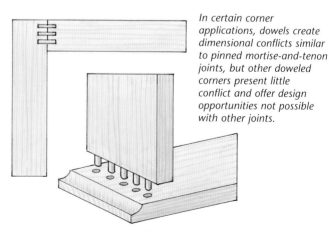

Using dowels

It makes sense to build with dowels when joinery isn't a design feature and tension on the joint won't be in line with the dowels. Doweled parts usually butt together, so with no extending tenons to calculate, doweling simplifies cutting parts to length. Doweling requires only that the parts meet squarely and the holes align straight. However, it is important that hole placements are accurate to within the thickness of a few sheets of paper.

A number of proprietary doweling jigs on the market aid accurate drilling. Their features and abilities vary, but their main function is to carry a bushing that fits the drill bit and guides it 90° to the wood surface. Such jigs usually locate holes along a line.

A row of holes for dowels is laid out along a board's edge or end. Commercial jigs locate the hole by automatically centering it or by referencing from one face of the board while an adjustment sets the hole's location in relation to the board's side or edge.

Jigs have index marks to set the bushing center at hole locations marked along the length. Mating hole locations are transferred to the mating part during layout by squaring marks across the edge or by markers called dowel centers, which are used after drilling the first part. Some jigs position the bushing to drill a mating hole by indexing from a dowel inserted in the first hole. Others hold parts in alignment to drill mating holes in pairs. Few commercial jigs allow for drilling in a board's face or for more than one or two holes at a time; shop made jigs are more adaptable and efficient for carcass joinery.

A steady hand can make a simple through dowel joint by freehand drilling into both parts while they're clamped in assembly position. The dowel ends that show at the surface can be kerfed

and wedged, plugged, or covered by mouldings. Some doweling is possible on the drill press, but it's often easier to use its accuracy to drill a scrap block of dense wood for a single-use jig to guide a hand-held drill.

Joint Strength

Dowels used in a doorframe are strong against shearing, but not a good choice in a drawer face where tension pulls in line with the dowels.

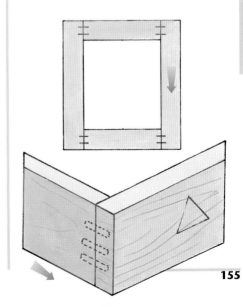

Laying Out and Transferring Hole Positions

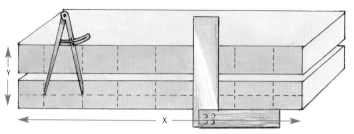

The hole spacing is marked out along the x plane and squared across to a mating part while jigs or machines are set to repeat the y location.

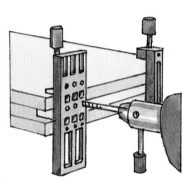

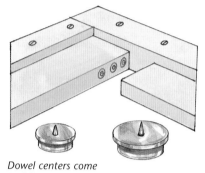

Some jigs index the mating hole from a dowel inserted in the first hole (above), while others position the parts to drill mating holes at the same time (below).

Dowel centers come in different hole sizes and work best to mark the drilling locations in mating parts if a temporary frame is used to guide the parts into position.

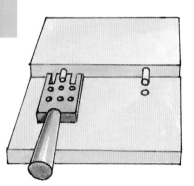

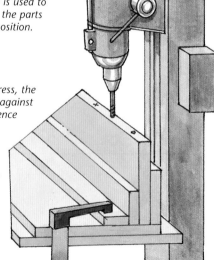

On the drill press, the part registers against an auxiliary fence which locates and repeats the y location of the dowel holes that are spaced out along the x plane.

Dowel Hole Accuracy

Holes not 90°

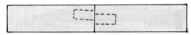

Holes accidentally referenced
from opposite faces

*Both dowel holes
must be drilled
90° to the wood
surface so the
dowel will seat; for
good alignment,
dowels should be
referenced from
the same face
or centered.*

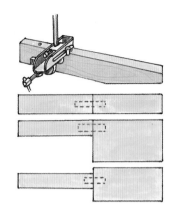

*A self-centering jig with
integral bushings drills
only in the center of the
board's edge and won't
align the faces of
different-sized stock.*

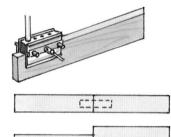

*A single-hole edge indexing jig
carrying interchangeable
bushings registers from the
same face of both parts and
will align them flush unless the
registration is readjusted to
create an offset.*

Shop made Doweling Jigs

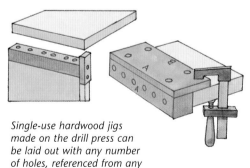

*Single-use hardwood jigs
made on the drill press can
be laid out with any number
of holes, referenced from any
face, and are held in place
by brads or clamps.*

*To compensate for
any deviation from
90° in a shop made
jig's holes, always
drill mating parts
from the opposite
jig side by jig design
or by reversing
the fence.*

*A simple self-centering jig could be
adapted like any shop jig to carry
some types of commercial steel
drill bushings sold as spares.*

Reinforced width miter

Regardless of the tools used, the basic procedure for doweling is the same. Choose a dowel diameter and matching drill bit a third to half the stock thickness. Cut the stock to size and mark a centered or offset hole location within the y plane of one part's thickness. For a shop made jig, do this layout on stock matched to the parts.

Extend a line paralleling the x plane from the marked y point and lay out a row of holes along it, spacing the dowels according to their purpose of aligning, reinforcing, or substituting for mortise and tenon. Dowels for alignment are minimal; as tenons, they should be placed together at least a diameter apart so the walls aren't weak.

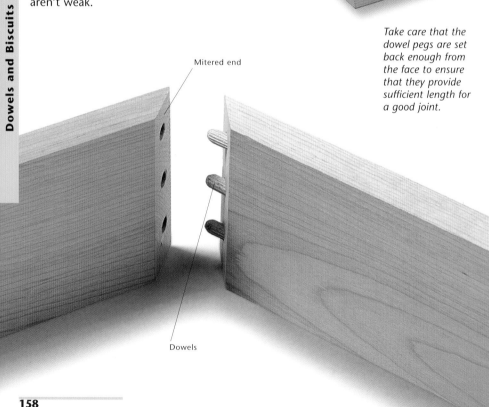

Take care that the dowel pegs are set back enough from the face to ensure that they provide sufficient length for a good joint.

Mitered end

Dowels

Reinforced Width Miter

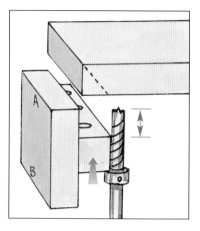

1 Cut the parts to final length, make a jig for drilling inside the miter, set the stop to drill the chosen depth, and tap the jig on with brads.

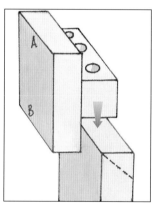

2 Drill the mating holes in the second part from the opposite side of the jig, then saw the miter across all the parts without removing any length.

3 Brush glue in the holes and on the dowels, inserting them in one part and using a block to close the miter's edge while clamping down on the dowels.

Drill Bits and Stops A bit has to be capable of positive location and staying on course in both end and face grain, preventing tear-out in face grain, and leaving an easy-to-measure flat-bottomed hole. In addition, the bit's ability to pull wood chips away from the cutting edge is critical to reducing any build-up of heat. Drill bits that meet these criteria are brad-point and Forstner bits.

Reinforced Width Miter

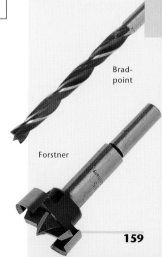

Brad-point

Forstner

Moulded-edge carcass joint

The doweling method is determined by where the holes are needed in the parts and the easiest available tool to drill them accurately. Board edges are easy to drill on the drill press, but long cabinet sides are better suited to a portable drill and jig.

There are a number of varying methods for transferring the hole locations to mating parts. For a single-hole doweling jig or drill press, square the marks across to all the parts. For jigs that index off an inserted dowel, or jigs that align mating parts for simultaneous drilling, mark only the first set of holes for dowel centers. A shop-made jig can carry the entire layout and eliminate marking.

The dowel pegs will minimize any tendency to warp, with shop-made dowels, cut flutes in the pegs to allow the free passage of glue.

Dowels and Biscuits

Moulded-Edge Carcass Joint

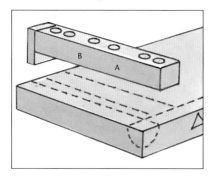

1 Cut the part to be moulded to length and width, then map out the moulding and side placement to make a jig, spacing the holes closer together near the edges at each end.

Multi-spur bits are used for the drill press, and Jennings or Irwin pattern bits for the brace. Twist drills can be used for doweling, but the bit will shred face grain and may not center easily. An indent punched at the mark provides a little starting guidance.

2 Drill the carcass parts, making sure to index the jig from the same face, and reverse the fence to drill mating parts from the opposite side of the jig.

3 Cut the moulding, brush glue in the holes and tap in the dowels, using a height block to stop them just short of the hole bottom for a glue reservoir.

Multi-spur

Jennings pattern

Irwin pattern

161

Doweled framing joint

U sed as tenons, dowels should enter each mating part to a minimum depth of one and a half times the dowel diameter. Used for alignment, dowels can be shorter. Set a bit depth stop or the drill press stop to drill the hole deep enough for the dowel plus a slight glue reservoir.

Use the drill press or index the jig on the marks to drill the holes. Put the bit into the jig hole or bushing, before starting to drill, occasionally backing the running drill bit partly out of the hole to clear the flutes. Don't press down hard when nearing the stop, or it could slip up the shank of the bit.

Dowels and Biscuits

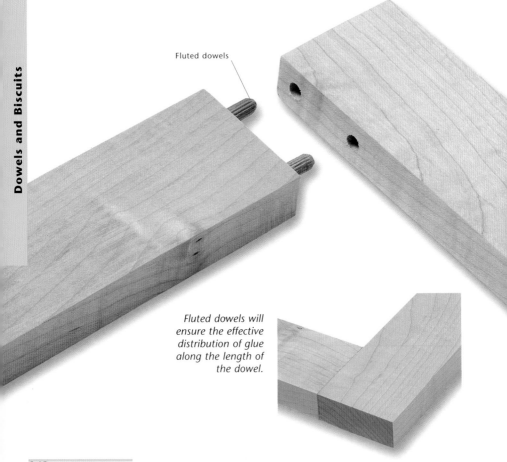

Fluted dowels

Fluted dowels will ensure the effective distribution of glue along the length of the dowel.

Doweled Framing Joint

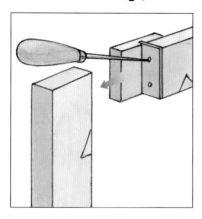

1 Make a layout template that substitutes dowels and holes at the mortise-and-tenon position, then mark the dowel hole positions on rails and stiles with an awl.

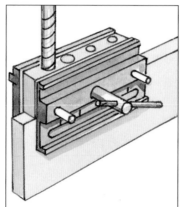

2 To drill, index a doweling jig to the awl marks, inserting a shim against the wood's face if necessary to adjust the holes off the center of the *y* plane.

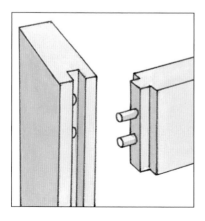

3 Complete any remaining milling on the frame, whether grooves, rabbets, moulding, or haunches. Glue in the dowels and assemble.

To gauge dowel hole depth on a portable drill or brace, put a depth stop on the bit. Stops range from a piece of masking tape with an extending tab that sweeps the surface when the drill reaches the right depth, to steel collars held on by set screws. A Fuller countersink and a stop in the drill press drills a hole to the right depth and countersinks a glue reservoir in one operation.

Wood stop collar

Fuller countersink and stop collar

ABOUT BISCUIT JOINERY

Biscuit, or plate, joinery is a relatively new method for joining wood. It was developed to join materials like plywood and particleboard, but it has also become popular for joining solid wood.

Biscuits are thin, football-shaped pieces of compressed beech that join parts in the same way as loose tenons, dowels, or splines. Most biscuit joints are made by a portable electric tool called a plate joiner, which looks like a small right angle grinder with a carbide-toothed saw blade. The machine's main function is to plunge its blade to a calibrated depth into mating parts. Each semicircular kerf left in the parts by the blade encloses half the biscuit.

Biscuits themselves are made from compressed beech cut so the grain runs diagonally across them for strength. There are three standard sizes used by all machines (0, 10, 20) and certain machines can use larger biscuits or kerf for smaller, thinner biscuits using a nonstandard blade. Spline cutters used in routers or laminate trimmers can rout kerfs for special round biscuits.

Biscuits require water-based glues like aliphatic resins. By design, the moisture swells the slightly compressed biscuit, tightening it in the kerf.

The number of plate joiners on the market offers woodworkers a choice of features over an extended price range. The most important considerations here are the ease and range of fence adjustment, the range of fence angles, and the miter indexing method.

Most biscuit joinery references the machine's fence against the wood's face or end to position the kerf. The distance between the blade and the fence has some adjustment. The most versatile blade height adjustment uses a rack and pinion to move the fence up and down in relation to the blade, although in practice an infinite number of positions aren't often needed, given common wood thicknesses.

On all machines the fence references at 90° to the surface being kerfed to make most parallel, T, or L joints, and at 45° to end or edge miters. Some fences also reference at any angle in between, a handy feature for joining beveled work. The machine also references off its flat base.

A biscuit joint is quickly made by a dedicated hand power tool.

About Biscuit Joiners

The retractable spring-loaded base of the plate joiner encloses a small circular saw blade that is plunged into the wood to various depth settings, making arced kerfs that fit the biscuits.

Types of Plate Joiner Fences

The plate joiner fence (in this case a fixed-angle fence) indexes to a mark on the wood, referencing off one face to cut the biscuit's kerf in the adjacent face.

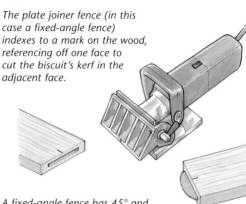

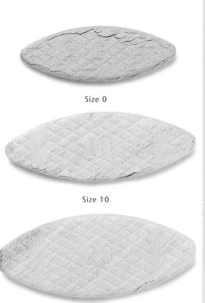

Size 0

Size 10

Size 20

All plate joiners cut kerfs for the three basic biscuit sizes; other sizes, shapes, and types are for specific joiner brands or router-cut slots.

A fixed-angle fence has 45° and 90° sides and reverses to cut miters, aligning the inside faces of the joint if the fence angles up from the blade.

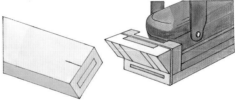

A fixed-angle fence that angles down over the blade indexes from the outside of a miter so the outside surfaces align.

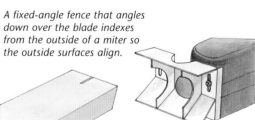

A variable-angle fence on the joiner lets it kerf for biscuits in bevel joints that aren't 45° or 90°.

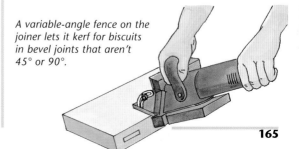

Flush framing joint

Biscuit joints are so simple to make it's not surprising they've become popular. The layout doesn't require precision, machine set-up is simple, and the joint is cut in seconds. Biscuit machines are very safe. The base or the wood always encloses the blade, and retractable pins or rubber spots on the base resist slippage during kerfing.

The basic joinery procedure is the same regardless of the type of joint. Cut the parts to size and clamp or hold them in assembly position to mark the location of each biscuit across the joint with a soft pencil. Since biscuits have a little side-to-side play in the kerf for joint adjustment during glue-up, marking doesn't have to be precise.

Size 20 biscuit

Cut slot

The flush framing joint is virtually the fastest joint there is to construct. When inserting a dry biscuit into a slot, the biscuit should be a snug fit across the thickness.

Flush Framing Joint

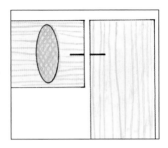

1 Cut the parts to length and place them in assembly position, then choose the largest biscuit that fits the stock and mark its center across the part with a soft pencil.

TRADE SECRETS

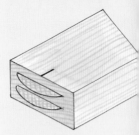

Double Biscuits
For extra strength or thick stock, use double biscuits by marking both sides of the wood and setting the fence to cut part way down the thickness from each side.

2 Adjust the 90° fence up or down to center the blade in the stock. Set the machine for the biscuit size, index on the marks, and plunge in the blade.

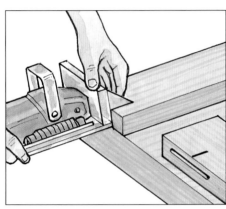

Referencing Marks Very few biscuits are necessary to reinforce and align width joints; use the benchtop or 90° fence to reference the machine to the marks.

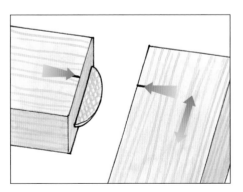

3 Spread glue in the kerfs and surrounding wood but not on the biscuit, insert a biscuit, and assemble the joint using the play in the kerfs to align the parts.

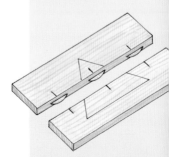

Flush Framing Joint

Biscuited T orientation

Clamp down parts for kerfing, or set up a backstop to keep them from sliding back when the blade is pushed into the wood. Dust usually ejects to the right, so start on the right and move left to keep referencing surfaces clean if the machine does not have dust collection.

Special expensive glue bottles are available to apply glue to the kerfs, but a simple flux brush works fine. Remember that glue swells the biscuits, so apply glue only to the parts to be joined, not the biscuits, and have clamps ready. Move quickly once they're inserted.

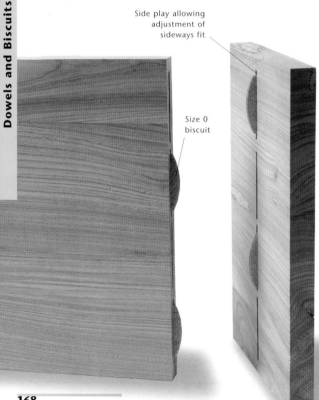

Side play allowing adjustment of sideways fit

Size 0 biscuit

Use water-based glue to ensure that the biscuit swells to create a strong joint.

Biscuited T Orientation

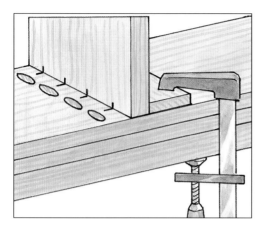

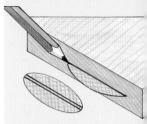

Kerfs To fine-tune kerf depth, mark a biscuit, reverse it and re-mark; adjust the machine so the first line doesn't show when the biscuit is reinserted, and there is a small gap between the lines.

1 Clamp a guide across one part to line up the other in position so a row of biscuits can be laid out and marked on both parts.

2 Set or remove the tool's fence so the nose is square to the base; align the base vertically against the straight guide and kerf to the marks, keeping within the joining part's outline.

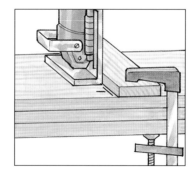

Sizes Layout spacing and the biscuit size to use depend on the wood's dimensions and the purpose of the joint. Wood thickness has to be more than half the biscuit width for kerfs into the face, or the blade will come through the back face. More or bigger biscuits give more glue surface and increase strength but aren't necessary if the biscuits are only for alignment.

3 Clamp down the second part and use the benchtop to reference the mating kerfs in the stock thickness at the index marks. Then spread glue, insert biscuits, assemble, and clamp.

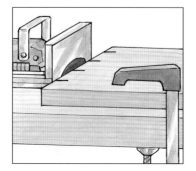

Biscuited T Orientation

169

Offset L joint

Whether a joint is marked across its inside or outside depends on the type of joint and the referencing method being used: either the straight or angled fence or the base of the machine. Initial marks can be squared around or extended so the machine's index mark is easy to line up to them during kerfing.

The use of a packing piece under the jointer makes it possible to insert a biscuit at any height when using two different thickness of material.

Slots cut in center of timber

Size 10 biscuit

Offset L Joint

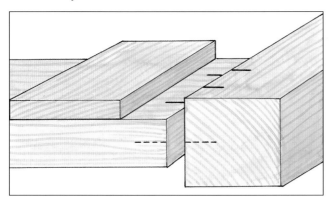

1 Mark for biscuits and stack a shim the same thickness as the offset on the thin part, using the stack to set the fence to cut at the center of the thin stock.

2 Place the shim on the thin stocks under the fence to cut mating kerfs at the index marks.

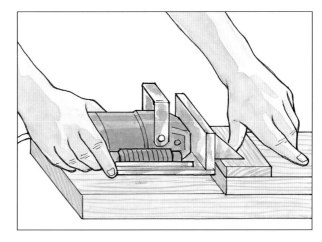

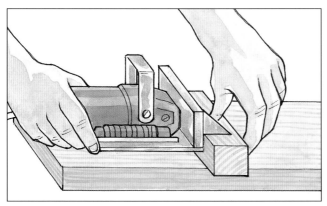

3 Without changing the blade height setting, kerf the thicker part at the index marks. Then spread glue, assemble, and clamp.

Using wood screws

Creating joints with screws isn't the conventional philosophy of woodworking, but screws make butted or lapped joints and reinforce or pin traditional joints. Screwed joints can be taken apart and, if glued, bond well without clamps.

The traditional woodworking screw with its flat, oval, or round head has been joined by hardened-steel production screws. These screws have flat heads if designed for particleboard, or self-sinking "bugle" heads if they're designed for driving into softwoods, like drywall screws that have crossed over to woodworking from the building trades.

Types of Screws

Steel screws are hardened for power driving with a drill/driver. They don't use the wood screw's typical slot drive but take advantage of the extra gripping power of Phillips, square, or combination drives. Hardening makes screws brittle and, especially without a pilot hole, liable to break off in hardwoods. Soft brass wood screws have a similar problem that is remedied by pre-tapping the hole with a steel wood screw, then replacing it with a brass wood screw.

Threads on wood screws climb around the screw at a lower angle than threads on hardened screws. The higher lead angle pulls hardened screws in quicker with fewer revolutions. The hardened screws' deeper threads, especially on particleboard screws, create a tenacious grip that is less likely to strip out of the wood.

Besides the lustrous beauty of brass, bronze, or stainless steel over the hardened screw's dull blackened steel, wood screws always have the advantage of a bare shank section close to the head. This lets the screw spin in the wood anchor part and allows the threads to pull the front piece up tight against it. When threads are engaging both parts, any space between the parts won't close. The screw has to be backed out and the parts clamped together for joining.

Screw Drives

The common types of screw drives and drivers in use are the straight slot, crossed Phillips, square drive, and a hybrid called combi, recex, or squarex.

Straight Crossed Square
slot Phillips drive

Screw Heads

The common wood screw is mild steel or brass and has one of three head types, either flat, oval, or round.

Bugle

The three basic head styles of hardened steel screws are flat, bugle, or trim head for finishing work.

Flat Trim head

Low profile pan heads, head washer, and oversized washer heads bring a flat and increasingly large surface to bear on the wood.

Washer head

Screws for Woodwork

The confirmat is a firm-holding assembly screw for cabinets of plywood or particleboard; it requires a pilot hole made by a special three-step drill bit.

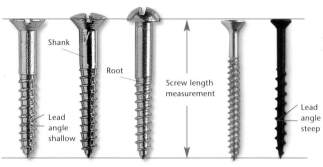

Shank

Root

Screw length measurement

Lead angle shallow

Lead angle steep

Nibs

Auger points

The different heads of wood screws sit flush or proud, the shanks are long and bare, threads climb the root at a low angle, and the root tapers to the tip.

Production screws sit flush or just below the wood surface, have nearly straight profiles, and double or single high-lead threads most of their length.

To save time, some production screws have auger points or nibs under the head so that during driving the screw drills its own pilot hole or sinks itself into the wood.

Using Wood Screws

Pilot Holes and Countersinks

The shank portion of the stepped wood screw pilot hole should extend through one piece so the threads will pull in the other piece and tighten the parts.

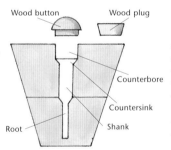

Wood button

Wood plug

Counterbore

Countersink

Root

Shank

The pilot hole for hardened steel screws should be the same as the root diameter, or slightly larger with a clearance hole for hardwoods.

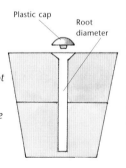

Plastic cap

Root diameter

Moveable depth stop collar

A wood screw countersink can match a single screw size or adjust for a range of sizes with a tapered bit and moveable collars.

Size 8 wood screw drill bit and countersink

When drilling for hinge hardware, Vix bits in three different sizes have a drill bit enclosed by a spring-loaded nose that helps to center the pilot hole.

Finishing washers in brass, black, or nickel plate hide the hole, increase the bearing area, and create a counter-sink for the screw head above the wood's surface.

173

Assembly fasteners and reinforcements

Using hardware to strengthen or hold furniture together is a technique as old as furniture itself. Today's hardware for the home-woodworker is more sophisticated and varied than the iron straps of old, and more cost-effective.

Joining with assembly hardware often involves nothing more than locating holes, inserting the mating hardware, and adjusting it with a screwdriver or wrench. Plywood or laminated board cabinets butted together in "box" style construction sometimes use surface-mounted or partially concealed connectors to join the parts. Hardware that permits easy assembly makes cabinets and countertops easier to move in sections and join together on site.

In the home shop, as in manufacturing, butted and hardware-joined construction eliminates time spent fitting, gluing, and clamping on projects that are not worth a large investment, like shelving and storage for the garage. The builder simply finds and installs hardware that holds parts in the required orientation.

Threaded inserts

These cylindrical inserts come in several sizes of brass and steel with deep external wood threads that screw into a pilot hole, and internal machine threads in common sizes. Inserts are an improved version of the old captured nut technique, which mortised a nut into wood, adding metal thread to grip assembly hardware like bedrail bolts.

Fasteners, Hardware, and Knockdown Joints

Width and Length joints

Industry fasteners or "dog bones" (right) were designed to join laminated countertops from the underside on site, but are useful for other length and width joinery, or in place of clamps.

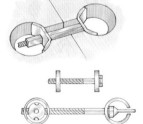

When inserted into a drilled hole, a special "keyhole" router bit cuts T-slotted keyholes (bottom) or routs a T-slot (below top) to house round screw heads for joints that can be disassembled.

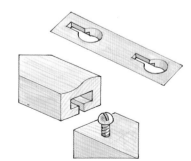

Another product inspired by industry is knock-down or site assembly hardware designed to be epoxied into (center and right) or to grip (left) biscuit joiner slots.

Surface–Mounted Hardware

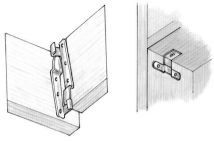

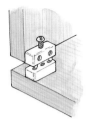

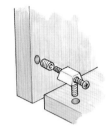

Plenty of serviceable but not particularly attractive interlocking hardware is available for most corner T or L joints.

Some joining hardware is based on the European cabinet making system of spacing a series of holes 32 millimeters on center, or by surface mounting with screws to assemble the joints.

Partially Concealed Connectors

Many systems imitate the action of draw-bored mortises and tenons by catching the protruding head of a special screw in an eccentric nut that is tightened to pull the joint home.

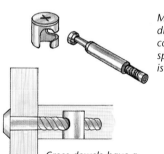

Cross dowels have a special threaded nut that is inserted into the part from below and adjusted so the screw threads engage the hole and pull the joint tight.

A relative of the cross dowel, the two-part connector bolt comes in two lengths and threads together from the insides of adjacent cabinets to anchor them.

"Locating dowels" use the 32 millimeter system of holes to thread into a part and line up with a mating housing nut that tightens over the dowel's head.

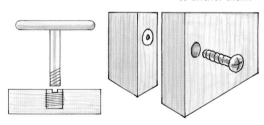

A T-tool or double-nutted bolt threads steel and brass inserts to provide strong internal machine screw threads.

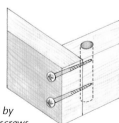

Joints made by plain wood screws into a board's end will hold better if the fragile end grain is replaced by the better screw-holding power of a dowel's long grain.

Tabletop Fasteners

Store-bought or homemade
tabletop buttons screw
underneath the top, sliding in
a groove in the apron with solid
wood expansion, while the round
desktop fastener is fine for
plywood (far right).

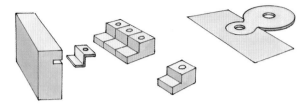

Cabinet Hangers

Light wall cabinets can be mounted
with interlocking steel hardware or
brass keyholes that fit over a
screwhead to minimize wall damage;
for heavier cabinets, use wood or metal
hanging rails.

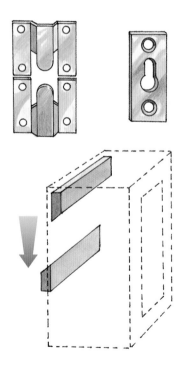

Bedrail Fasteners

For traditional
work, a square-
headed bedrail
bolt with its nut
mortised in from
the bedrail's
inside is covered
with a metal
cap, to decorate
and hide the
access hole.

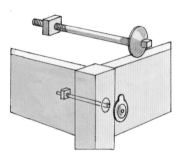

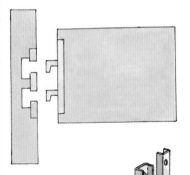

*Tapered sliding or
hooked bedrail hangers
are nicest when
mortised into the bedrail
end so they don't show,
and also work to hang
heavy cabinets.*

Corner Reinforcements

Plastic, steel, or brass reinforcements for every type of intersection are readily available in most hardware stores.

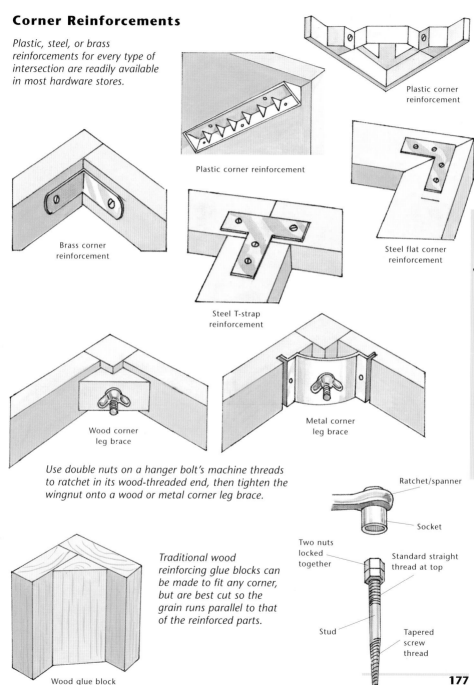

Plastic corner reinforcement

Plastic corner reinforcement

Brass corner reinforcement

Steel flat corner reinforcement

Steel T-strap reinforcement

Wood corner leg brace

Metal corner leg brace

Use double nuts on a hanger bolt's machine threads to ratchet in its wood-threaded end, then tighten the wingnut onto a wood or metal corner leg brace.

Ratchet/spanner

Socket

Traditional wood reinforcing glue blocks can be made to fit any corner, but are best cut so the grain runs parallel to that of the reinforced parts.

Two nuts locked together

Standard straight thread at top

Stud

Tapered screw thread

Wood glue block

177

Keyed tenon

Furniture that breaks down into its components is part of a tradition that includes Roman military campaign furniture and "traveling" medieval trestle tables that were designed to be moved on a daily basis. Woodworkers who enjoy the challenge of building all-wood structures that break down into smaller and lighter components will find the glueless knockdown joinery of old still useful today. The through keyed or tusked tenon is a strong, visible joint that resists racking but has to be integrated with the overall design. A sliding dovetail mechanically interlocks to hold a structure invisibly, plus it breaks down and easily reassembles, especially when it's waxed.

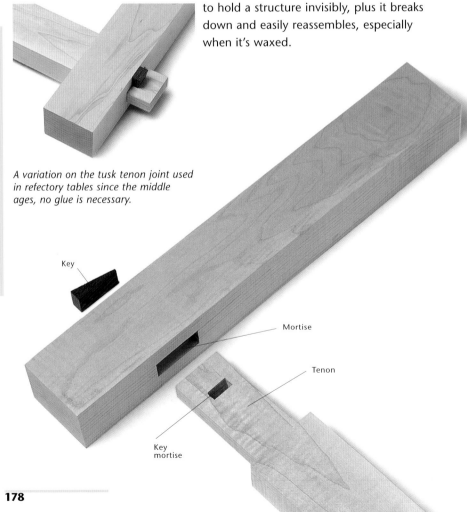

A variation on the tusk tenon joint used in refectory tables since the middle ages, no glue is necessary.

Key

Mortise

Tenon

Key
mortise

Keyed Tenon

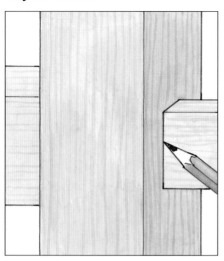

1 Make an overlong through tenon so it has some extending material that can be mortised, insert the tenon through, and mark its face where it exits its mortise.

2 Lay out a mortise on the tenon, starting it just inside the line on the tenon face and leaving enough material to prevent short grain when the mortise is cut.

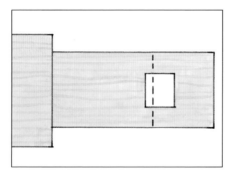

Sliding Dovetails
To make moving or shipping easier, use unglued sliding dovetails to break bulky furniture into components, as in separating a desk into its modesty panel, and cabinets and top.

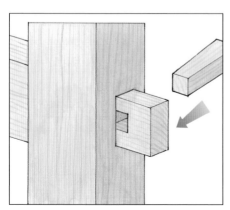

3 Make a key whose outside face tapers slightly, and insert it through the mortise in the tenon so it bears against the upright and then pulls the tenon tight.

Half-dovetail tenon

For making constructions that can readily be dismantled and reassembled, the dovetail tenon is one of a small group of versatile joints (see Variations, page 181). The tenon is cut in the conventional way, but with side shoulders only, before the dovetail is marked, (always on its lower edge) and cut. The mortise is cut to the full width of the tenon and afterward opened from the outer end to the angle of the tenon dovetail. When wedged finally, the joint is very rigid provided that the timber used is relatively wide and the tenon is a close fit in the mortise for good lateral support.

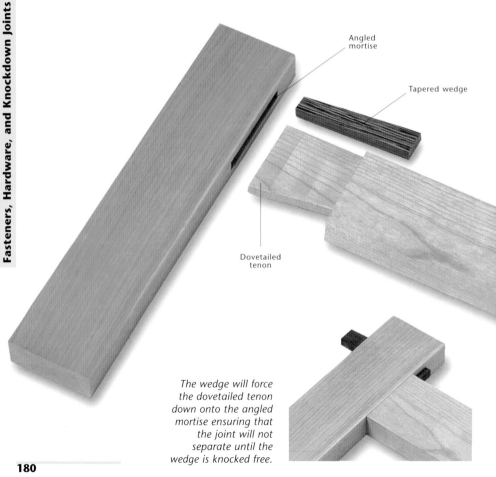

Angled mortise

Tapered wedge

Dovetailed tenon

The wedge will force the dovetailed tenon down onto the angled mortise ensuring that the joint will not separate until the wedge is knocked free.

Half-Dovetail Tenon

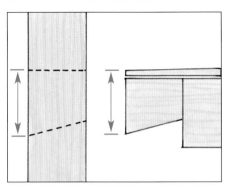

1 Lay out the through mortise for a half-dovetail tenon so its bottom end angles to the dovetail and the exiting side is long enough to include the thickness of a wedge.

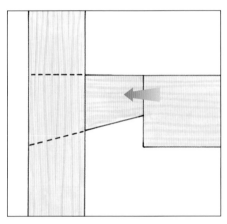

2 Make sure that the tenon can enter the mortise when its top edge is aligned with the top end of the mortise.

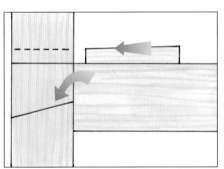

3 Insert the tenon and drop it down to fit the angles together, then slide in the tapered wedge, shaving it thinner until it stops flush with the tenon end.

VARIATIONS

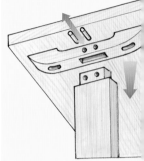

Blind Tenon
Removable pins in a blind tenon hold it tight but allow the furniture to be broken down for handling.

Tusked Tenon
When rails are thick enough, tusk a tenon with a vertical wedge following the same procedure outlined for a keyed tenon.

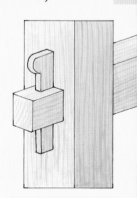

Half-Dovetail Tenon

EDGE AND SCARF JOINTS

The purpose of edge and scarf joints is to join individual boards into one wider or longer unit. There is little dimensional conflict, and because the parallel grain direction of their bonding surfaces makes a glue bond as strong as the wood itself, these joints require no interlocking joinery. However, there are methods to interlock such joints to reinforce them against certain types of stress, improve aesthetics, increase the gluing surface, or assist alignment and reduce slippage during gluing. But these refinements are just icing on an already substantial cake.

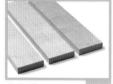

Plain butt glue joint   **page 26**

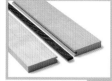

Splined joint   **page 29**

Tongue and groove   **page 31**

End-to-end scarf   **page 34**

Edge-to-edge scarf   **page 36**

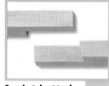

Squint butted scarf   **page 38**

LAPPED AND HOUSED JOINTS

Joint Selector

Lap joints are a simple family, suggesting their unique construction method, which reduces each part to half its thickness or width at the joint and laps one part over the other. They are also called half-laps or halving joints. Laps appear in L, T, and crossed orientations. Housed joints use the same flat-bottomed milled elements as lap joints, but one part encloses or houses the other in an L or T orientation to serve some specific construction needs. Both these families can be modified.

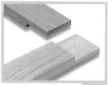

End lap   **page 45**

Center lap   **page 48**

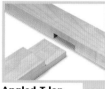

Angled T-lap   **page 51**

Jigged edge lap   **page 53**

Box joint on the table saw   **page 55**

Full housing by hand   **page 60**

Full housing on the table saw   **page 62**

Routed housed rabbet   **page 64**

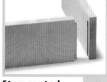

Stop-routed housed rabbet   **page 66**

MORTISE-AND-TENON

The mortise-and-tenon joint has been an effective method of joining wood at right angles since ancient times. Its basic form and variations continue to serve as a primary method for joining frames, leg assemblies, and carcass skeletons.

A tenon is a long tongue that fits into a pocket, or mortise, in a mating part. Like lap joints, the mortise-and-tenon is glued cheek to cheek, but unlike lap joints, where one long-grain cheek is glued to the other, the mortise-and-tenon doubles the gluing surface by bonding two tenon face cheeks to two long-grain mortise cheeks. Also like lap joints, the cheeks are glued cross-grain, so some dimensional conflict is inherent in mortise-and-tenon joints as it is in laps.

Basic mortise-and-tenon　page **76**

Open slot mortise on a radial-arm saw　page **80**

Through mortise by hand　page **82**

Angled mortise and tenon　page **84**

Through wedged tenon　page **87**

Draw-bored tenon　page **89**

Angled tenon and shoulder　page **91**

Slip, or loose, tenon　page **93**

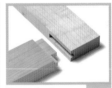

Haunched tenon　page **96**

Sloped haunched tenon　page **98**

Mortise-and-tenon with panel groove　page **100**

Mortise-and-tenon for a rabbeted frame　page **102**

Mortise-and-tenon for a moulded frame　page **104**

MITERS AND BEVELS

Miters and bevels are cuts made at angles other than 90°. Aesthetically, miters or bevels can unify a shape visually by continuing the line of grain around it. Structurally, miters add softening facets and bridge the gap between squares and circles. The terms "miter" and "bevel" sometimes interchange. An important distinction is that a bevel cut is not perpendicular to the face of the wood, whereas a miter is either an exact 45° cut (even if it's a bevel) or a general term for an angled cut.

Frame miter by hand	page **112**

Feathered miter on a radial-arm saw	page **114**

Lap miter	page **116**

Housed rabbet miter	page **118**

Locked miter	page **120**

Waterfall joint	page **122**

Rabbet miter	page **124**

Compound miter by machine	page **126**

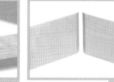

Compound miter by hand	page **128**

DOVETAILS

Often considered the hallmark of fine workmanship in wood, dovetails are interlocking joints with a great deal of mechanical strength. The dovetail is constructed with an angled male part shaped like the joint's name which fits into a similarly shaped female socket. In its best known configuration at an end to face corner, a dovetail joint is a series of tails fit into a series of sockets. The parts between socket are called pins. They fit like interlocking tenons into the spaces between the tails. The widening tail braces the joint against tension, adding great mechanical strength to the long-grain glue surface between the tails and pins.

Through dovetail	page **134**

Half-blind dovetail	page **138**

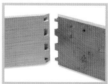

Blind mitered dovetail	page **140**

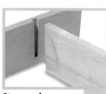

Stopped tapered dovetail by hand	page **142**

Joint Selector

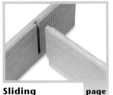

| Sliding dovetail drawer joint | page **144** | Dovetail keys | page **146** | Butterfly keys | page **148** | Dovetail splines | page **150** |

DOWELS AND BISCUITS

Modernized versions of common joints have developed over time to speed manufacturing or accommodate new materials. Dowel joints and biscuit joinery are both by-products of industry. They make quick work of joinery by eliminating time-consuming fitting of joined elements, and are alternatives that should find an appropriate place in every woodworker's repertoire.

Joint Selector

| Reinforced width miter | page **158** | Moulded-edge carcass joint | page **160** | Doweled framing joint | page **162** |

| Flush framing joint | page **166** | Biscuited T orientation | page **168** | Offset L joint | page **170** |

FASTENERS, HARDWARE, AND KNOCKDOWN JOINTS

There are occasions when temporary joinery is more convenient for large and restless pieces of furniture, or no joinery at all may be more suited to the purpose or status of the structure. Woodworking accommodates these contingencies with joints that disassemble and reassemble, and with old standby screws and fasteners, and modern inventions that work without glue or that reinforce glued joinery.

| Keyed tenon | page **178** | Half-dovetail tenon | page **180** |

Glossary

Awl A pointed scribing tool used to mark layout lines. It works well with the grain, but has a tendency to fuzz up marks across the grain.

Beam The "handle" of a square or miter square as opposed to the blade, or the part of a marking gauge that holds the point.

Bending A tendency of wood to flex or the joint parts to pull away from each other under force on the side opposite an imaginary fulcrum.

Bevel A cut that is not 90° to a board's face, or the facet left by such a cut.

Biscuit A thin, flat oval of compressed beech that is inserted between two pieces of wood into mating saw kerfs made by a biscuit or plate jointing machine.

Bowing A lumber defect caused by drying. It makes the wood face bend up along its length like a rocker.

Box joint Another name for a fingerlap joint with straight, interlocking fingers.

Bridle joint A joint that combines features of both lap joints and mortise and tenon. It has a U-shaped mortise in the end of the board.

Butt joint Two flat facets of mating parts that fit flush together with no interlocking joinery.

Carcass The main body or frame of a piece of cabinet work.

Center lap A wide dado cut halfway into the thickness of a part to form half a frame lap joint.

Check A crack in wood material caused by drying, either just in the surface or in the end of the board so the fibers have separated.

Cheek The face of a tenon, center lap, or end lap, the long-grain walls of a mortise, or the long-grain mating surface of dovetails and their pins or box joint fingers.

Clamping blocks Blocks of wood that help distribute clamp force to the joint's gluing surfaces when correctly sized.

Combi drive A system for driving screws that incorporates more than one type of drive indentation in the screw head so it can be driven by several different drivers.

Combination square An all-metal, engineer-style square which can prove 90° and 45° angles. Its blade slides back and forth within the beam and can accommodate attachments like a centering head or a protractor.

Compound miter A cut where the blade path is not perpendicular to the wood's end or edge and the blade tilt is not 90° to the face.

Compression Force on wood that pushes fibers in on themselves, or a joint in on itself.

Confirmat An assembly screw used for cabinets of manmade sheet goods.

Coping Sawing a negative profile in one piece to fit the positive profile of another, usually in molding.

Counterbore A straight-sided drilled hole that recesses a screw head below the wood surface so a wood plug can cover it, or the bit which makes this hole.

Countersink A cone-shaped drilled hole whose slope angle matches the underside of a flat screw head and sinks it flush with the wood surface, or the tool that makes this hole.

Crooking A lumber-drying defect which causes a lateral bend in a board.

Cupping A drying defect where one side of the board shrinks across the grain more than the other, causing the board to curl in on itself like a trough.

Cutting gauge A device which carries a small knife for deep scoring of layout lines parallel to an edge or for cutting veneer into strips.

Dado A flat-bottomed, U-shaped milling cut of varying widths and depths but always running across the grain.

Dimensional conflict A situation where the long grain of the joined parts is glued or pinned perpendicularly and the natural fluctuation in the dimension of wood across the grain is restricted.

Double square A square which can prove 90° angles with its inside and outside corners, and whose blade sometimes slides within a metal beam so it can be used as a depth gauge or marking gauge.

Dovetail joint A traditional joint characterized by interlocking fingers and pockets shaped like its name. The joint has exceptional resistance to tension.

Dowel pin A small cylinder of wood that is inserted and glued between two parts in mating holes to create or reinforce a joint.

Doweling jig Any of a number of commercially available devices to assist placing and drilling dowel holes. It can be shopmade.

Draw-boring A technique by which a joint is pulled home when a peg is hammered through it into slightly offset holes in the parts.

Dressing The process of turning rough lumber into a smooth board with flat, parallel faces and straight, parallel edges and whose edges are square to the face.

Edge lap A notch into the edge of a board halfway across its width that forms half of an edge lap joint.

Element A basic shaped part of a joint, either a dado, rabbet, groove, pocket, or square or angled cut, or combinations and modifications of these.

End grain The grain at the end of a board which can be likened to a bundle of straws cut across their length; it shows

the tree's growth rings at various angles to the face of the board depending how the board was cut from the log. *See also* flatsawn and quartersawn.

End lap A rabbet across a board's face at its end which forms half of a frame lap joint in an L or T orientation (not to be confused with an end-to-end lap, or scarf joint).

Engineer's square A precision metal square with a fixed blade for proving 90°.

Face The widest part of the board as measured across the grain.

Fingerlap A specific joint of the lap family which has straight interwoven fingers; also called a box joint.

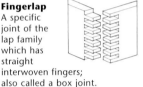

Flatsawn The most common cut of lumber where the growth rings run predominantly across the end of the board; or its characteristic grain pattern.

Grain pattern The visual appearance of the wood grain. Types of grain pattern include flat, straight, curly, quilted, rowed, mottled, crotch, cathedral, beeswing, or bird's-eye. For more on grain consult a wood specialty book.

Groove A flat-bottomed, U-shaped milling cut whose depth and width can vary, but which always runs with the grain.

Half lap Another name for a lap joint.

Half pin In dovetail joints, the two outside pins of a row, named not because they are half the width of the other but because they are angled only on one side.

Halving In lap joints a general term for a wide rabbet or dado cut halfway into the wood face or a notch cut in the edge; also another name for lap joints.

Hardwood Wood from broadleaf deciduous trees, no matter what the density (balsa is a hardwood).

Haunch A secondary shoulder cut into the edge of a tenon.

Housed A situation where one part is enclosed fully or partially by another, or a specific family of joints.

Housing A milled cut, usually a rabbet, dado, or groove, but sometimes a pocket, which encloses all or part of a mating piece.

Index A reference face, mark, or fence used to position a cut or a bit, or the act of alignment.

Jig Any shop-made or after-market device that assists in positioning and steadying the wood or tools.

Kerf The visible path of subtracted wood left by a sawblade.

Key An inserted joint-locking device, usually made of wood.

Keyhole bit A special T-shaped router bit that cuts an extruded T path inside the wood thickness; the shape lets screw heads into the wood, and the shanks slide along a groove that breaks the wood surface.

Knockdown joint A joint which is assembled without glue and can be disassembled and re-assembled if necessary.

Lap A type of cut, whether an end lap, center lap, or edge lap, used in lap joints. Also known as a halving.

Lap joint A type of joint made by removing half the thickness or width of the parts and lapping them over each other.

Length joint A joint which makes one longer wood unit out of two shorter ones by joining them end to end.

Lip A glued-on or overhanging border of wood.

Long grain The parallel fibers of the wood, like the length of a bundle of straws, that usually run parallel to the length of the board.

Marking gauge An adjustable device with a steel pin or knife which marks a single layout line parallel to a wood edge.

Marking knife Any knife, or a particular named style of knife, that is suitable for scribing layout lines.

Milling The process of removing material to leave a desired positive or negative profile in the wood.

Miter A generic term meaning mainly an angled cut across the face grain, or a specifically 45° cut across the face, end grain or along the grain. *See also* bevel.

Miter gauge A device that slides in a tabletop slot paralleling the blade of a tablesaw or bandsaw with a pivoting protractor head and fence to facilitate crosscutting at different angles.

Mortise The commonly rectangular or round pocket into which a mating tenon is inserted; mortises can be blind (stop inside the wood thickness), through, or open on one end.

Mortise marking gauge A device with two steel pins, which mark two layout lines parallel to a wood edge.

Notch A dado cut into the edge of wood that is part of an edge lap joint if it extends halfway into the wood width.

Open slot mortise A type of mortise made in the end of a board, used in a bridle joint.

Orientation The positional relationship between the parts in a joint—parallel, end to end or I, crossed, L, T and angled.

Over-bearing A type of router bit which carries the bearing above the cutter; a flush-trim over-bearing is particularly useful in template work because the template can be placed on top of the workpiece and the bit will cut the template's exact size.

Phillips drive A method of engaging a screw head with its mated driver by a cross-shaped indentation in the screw head.

Pilot hole A small drilled hole used as a guide and pressure relief for screw insertion, or to locate additional drilling work such as countersinking and counterboring.

Pin The part of a dovetail joint whose dovetail shape is on the end of the board and fits between the tails; a screw or dowel used to reinforce a joint.

Plate joiner A portable power tool dedicated to making slots or kerfs in the shape of an arc to fit biscuits in biscuit or plate joinery.

Pocket Any hole or socket of various shapes which fit mated joint parts.

Quartersawn A stable lumber cut where the growth rings on the board's end run more vertically across the end than horizontal and the grain on the face looks straight; also called straight-grained or riftsawn.

Rabbet A milled cut which leaves a flat step parallel to, but recessed from, the surface of the wood.

Racking The tendency of a joint to loosen and change its angle, usually in relation to a structure which compensates with a change in the other joints, like a rectangle changing to a parallelogram.

Rail The name given to the horizontal parts of a door or other frame.

Raker tooth A tooth type on some circular saw blades which is flat across its top so it can be used to make tolerably flat-bottomed grooves or waste material even by repeated passes across it.

Root The portion of a screw length below the head that has threads on it.

Scarf joint A joint that increases the overall length of wood by joining two pieces at their ends, gluing long bevels in their faces or edges.

Scribe To make layout lines or index marks with a knife or awl.

Shank The portion of a screw length below the head without threads on it.

Shear Force which pulls or pushes at a glueline or overloads a part to break it off.

Short grain Long grain whose fibers are cut across and left so short that the material becomes fragile and won't hold together.

Shoulder The perpendicular face of a step cut like a rabbet which bears against a mating joint part to stabilize the joint.

Sliding bevel A tool that has a changeable angle between its blade and beam. The blade length is also adjustable.

Slot drive A driving system for screws that mates the driver to a straight-grooved indentation across the head.

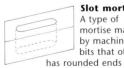

Slot mortise A type of mortise made by machine bits that often has rounded ends (which can be squared).

Softwood Wood from coniferous evergreen trees, no matter what the density (yew is a softwood).

Spline A flat, thin strip of wood that fits into mating grooves between two parts to reinforce the joint between them.

Split A situation where the wood material has broken along the grain. *See also* check.

Sprung joint An edge or width joint that has been planed slightly hollow to compensate for future moisture loss at the ends of the board which could shrink open the joint.

Square drive A Canadian screwdriving system that engages the screw by mating its driver to a square hole in the screw head.

Step collar A wooden or metal device placed on a drill bit to gauge the hole depth.

Stile The name of the vertical parts of a door or other frame.

Story pole A layout stick that holds the actual-sized project in section view.

Straight grain The grain pattern that results when the wood is quartersawn.

Tail The part of a dovetail joint whose dovetail shape is cut into the face of a board and which fits around the pins.

Taper A cut with the grain which gradually angles along the board edge instead of running parallel to it.

Tenon The male part of a mortise-and-tenon joint, commonly rectangular or

round, but not restricted to those shapes.

Tension Force on the joint or wood that pulls it in opposite directions.

Triangle marking A marking system that uses a simple triangle shape for marking wood to keep project parts sorted out.

Try miter A woodworker's testing device used for 45° angles.

Try square A woodworker's testing device for 90° angles that sometimes follows specifications requiring only its inside corner to be square.

Twisting A drying defect in lumber that causes it to twist so the faces at each end of the board are in a different plane.

Wedge Usually a thin slice of wood that is glued into a kerf in the end of a through tenon; sometimes interchanges with key.

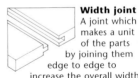

Width joint A joint which makes a unit of the parts by joining them edge to edge to increase the overall width of wood.

Winding sticks Two straight mated sticks that are placed on edge at opposite ends of a board and sighted across to prove the flatness of the lumber.

Wood movement The never-ending natural tendency of wood to expand and contract across the grain as its moisture content fluctuates in response to changes in relative humidity.

Index

Conversion terms

US	UK/Australia
angled joint	cross-halving joint
awl	bradawl
backsaw	tenon saw
bar clamp	sash clamp
brad	panel pin
carpenter's level	spirit level
carpenter's square	set square
C-clamp	G-clamp
chair rail	dado rail
cleat	batten
craft knife	scalpel
cross-peen hammer	pin hammer
dado	housing
DAR (dressed all round)	PAR (planed all round)
dovetail spline	dovetail slip feather tongue
dressed lumber	planed timber
hardware	fittings
hex key	Allen key
inside corner	internal corner
keyhole saw	pad saw
knock-down furniture	flat-pack furniture
lumber	timber
milled lumber	moulded timber
mineral spirits	white spirit
mortise	mortice
outside corner	external corner
quarter-round moulding	quadrant beading
rabbet	rebate
rule	ruler
spade bit	flat bit
splined joint	cross-tongue joint
squint-butted scarf joint	half-lapped scarf joint
utility knife	Stanley knife
vise	vice
wall anchor	wall plug
wallboard	plasterboard
white glue	PVA
wire brad	veneer pin
wrench	spanner

Index/Conversion Terms